DECODING THE PROPHET JEREMIAH

MARK BILTZ

CHARISMA
HOUSE

Most Charisma House Book Group products are available at special quantity discounts for bulk purchase for sales promotions, premiums, fund-raising, and educational needs. For details, call us at (407) 333-0600 or visit our website at www.charismahouse.com.

DECODING THE PROPHET JEREMIAH by Mark Biltz
Published by Charisma House
Charisma Media/Charisma House Book Group
600 Rinehart Road, Lake Mary, Florida 32746

Unless otherwise noted, all Scripture quotations are taken from the King James Version of the Bible.

Scripture quotations marked ESV are from the Holy Bible, English Standard Version. Copyright © 2001 by Crossway Bibles, a division of Good News Publishers. Used by permission.

Scripture quotations marked NKJV are taken from the New King James Version®. Copyright © 1982 by Thomas Nelson. Used by permission. All rights reserved.

Visit the author's website at elshaddaiministries.us or www. Biltzbook.com.

Library of Congress Cataloging-in-Publication Data:
An application to register this book for cataloging has been submitted to the Library of Congress.

The fateful lives and times during the prophet Jeremiah are not dissimilar to those of today. Author and compassionate prophetic teacher Mark Biltz continues his legacy of bringing light to often hard-to-understand Bible precepts, patterns, and shadows. Through his excellent work in *Decoding the Prophet Jeremiah*, Biltz excavates the ancient paths onto which Jeremiah directed Israel, deciphering them into the vital road map for our equipping and entering into God's kingdom age. Perhaps today's believers will take to heart the words of direction and warning that were widely disregarded or defied in Jeremiah's day. Biltz's wonderful book will show you how, and better still, why.

—Caz Taylor
Prophetic Teacher and Author
Salem Media Group, San Diego broadcaster

Jeremiah is one of my favorite prophets. His tenacity and zeal to speak the truth of God are evident throughout the Book of Jeremiah. However, when I read the Book of Jeremiah, I find it hard to follow, as dates, people, and events do not harmonize at times, leaving the reader somewhat confused. Jeremiah's writings reflect the chaos that was ruling the Israelites in that era. It did not make much sense on the timing of the chapters. It seems as if all the chapters were tossed in the air and then organized in the order in which they landed.

Pastor Mark Biltz, was able to put the entire book in a chronological order of events and people. I have no doubt that the Holy Spirit of the living God has poured down knowledge according to the scripture Jeremiah 33:3, "Call to me and I will answer you, and will tell you great and hidden things that you have not known" (ESV). It is obvious that the Lord has anointed Pastor Mark's mind to write this book, *Decoding the Prophet Jeremiah*. It is an outstanding resource for those who seek a deeper understanding of the writing of the prophet Jeremiah.

Meanwhile, for a researcher like me, it is a must-read. This book gave me a clearer landscape of the scripture and better understanding of events that reshaped the Israelites. I am grateful for Pastor Mark's knowledge shared through the journey of decoding the prophet Jeremiah.

—Rev. Haitham Besmar
Ordained Bishop through Church of God
Cleveland, Tennessee

The sages of Israel declared that no man is to enter the Paradise unless his stomach is filled with meat and wine. Pastor Biltz has given us a feast in this masterful publication. The book captures the great puzzle of Israel's past, present, and future in a relevant message that parallels the body of Messiah today. I was deeply impacted by the words of Pastor Biltz as a new "weeping prophet" of our generation.

—Rabbi Itzhak Shapira
Ahavat Ammi Ministries

DECODING THE PROPHET JEREMIAH

International Standard Book Number: 978-1-62999-728-5
E-book ISBN: 978-1-62999-729-2

20 21 22 23 24 —987654321
Printed in the United States of America

THIS BOOK ON THE WRITINGS OF JEREMIAH IS
DEDICATED TO ALL THOSE WHO ATTEND EL SHADDAI
MINISTRIES LOCALLY AND TO THE THOUSANDS WHO
LIVESTREAM OUR SERVICES EVERY SHABBAT FROM ALL
AROUND THE WORLD AND HELP US TO TAKE TORAH
TO THE NATIONS! THIS ENDEAVOR COULD NEVER
HAVE BEEN ACCOMPLISHED WITHOUT THE SUPPORT
RECEIVED FROM EACH AND EVERY ONE OF YOU. I AM
SO GRATEFUL FOR ALL THE ENCOURAGING EMAILS
AND PHONE CALLS, THE KIND CARDS, AND THE LOVING
LETTERS RECEIVED OVER THE YEARS FROM ALL OVER
THE GLOBE. MAY THE LORD BLESS ALL OF YOU!

CONTENTS

ACKNOWLEDGMENTS

I HAVE TO ACKNOWLEDGE Rabbi Itzhak Shapira, founder of Ahavat Ammi Ministries, for inspiring me during the writing of this work. You would not believe what happened! I love the prophet Jeremiah. He has to be one of my favorites. I was at home in my office when Rabbi Shapira called me from Israel. He was all excited and told me that he had finally acquired something he had been looking for forever. He had obtained a four-hundred-year-old scroll of the Book of Jeremiah! I couldn't believe it! I told him, "No way!" and that I was writing my next book on the Book of Jeremiah. I even told him I had spent six months of the previous year teaching every week from it, going through the whole book. He said, "No way!" Then he told me that he had just finished reading Jeremiah 31 at the Western Wall in Israel and doing a video commentary there at the Western Wall Plaza. I told him, "No way!" It just so happened that when he called me, I was currently working on that very chapter—Jeremiah 31.

I asked him if he could please send me an image of the scroll or an opened page so I could include the picture of it in this book.

He said he would be glad to help. Can you imagine holding a scroll of Jeremiah that is over four hundred years old? That's older than the Declaration of Independence by 150 years! Holding or even touching a scroll of Jeremiah that old would be mind-boggling, let alone being able to have it in your possession and owning it. A few hours after we hung up, I got an email from him. It totally blew me away! He said the Lord told him to donate it to me, and he was sending it the next day. Three days later at my doorstep I received the most unbelievable package in the entire world! I carefully pulled the scroll out of the box and took off the velvet cover protecting the scroll. There I was with tears in my eyes, actually holding a four-hundred-year-old scroll of Jeremiah. The Spirit of God that moved on Jeremiah was moving on me, and I could hardly wait to infuse that same Spirit into this book so that the Lord would give you His heart as we dig deeper into one of my favorite prophets—Jeremiah.

Here's a picture of the ancient Jeremiah scroll:

INTRODUCTION

THE WRITINGS OF the prophet Jeremiah have to be one of the most fascinating prophetic puzzles recorded in the Bible. Within the Book of Jeremiah the chapters are mixed up chronologically, as if the book was cut into pieces, thrown into the air, and pieced back together however they landed. To me this is representative of the chaotic times that Jeremiah lived in as he continuously warned the nation of Israel about the coming destruction of Jerusalem and the temple and the exile of God's people into Babylon. This was all due to their disobedience and their wanton disregard to the pleading of the God of their fathers to return to Him. Jeremiah is well known as the weeping prophet, and I believe that title is very appropriate because, as an ambassador for God, Jeremiah was properly representing grief and heartbreak over the coming judgment. God was brokenhearted as His own children spurned Him. Isaiah had warned them previously, as we find in the first chapter of his book where God declared that He brought up children and they rebelled against Him.[1]

Parents who genuinely love their teenage children may find it necessary to expel them if they continue to bring total chaos into the house—punching holes in the walls, being disrespectful, and acting totally rebellious. As a good Father, God found it necessary to expel His children from the Promised Land for seventy years until their punishment was complete.[2] Israel had to know that they really upset their Father this time after He not only expelled them from the House, but He then kicked them out of the country, vacated His own House, and even burnt it to the ground! They realized just how serious God was when He declared that they needed to keep and obey His commandments, statutes, and laws.[3] God had made good on the promises He gave them nearly a thousand years earlier, warning them that this would happen if they forsook Him and His laws. The good news for Israel, though, was that there were prophecies that they would return to the land and God would return to them as well. The Jews who remained faithful held tightly to the hope that God always keeps His covenant and His promises.

Hegel was right when he said the main thing we learn from history is that we do not learn from history.[4] In the first chapter of Ecclesiastes we read that everything that happened will happen again, and there is nothing new under the sun.[5] People are people, and while the faces may change over history, the actions of humanity are repeated over and over. With that said, as we "decode" the writings of Jeremiah, we will discover that history is repeating itself, and his ancient prophetic utterances are again ringing true in the ears of all who have ears to hear in our generation. Many will see the prophetic words from the Book of Jeremiah leaping off the pages within the Book of Revelation. The prophecy of the destruction of Babylon is just one of several found in both books.

To properly understand the Book of Jeremiah, we need to go back a few centuries and see the circumstances that led up to the condition warranting such a high level of divine retribution. Even in the midst of all the chaos, the mighty hand of God was orchestrating world events. He is often behind the scenes, just as in the Book of Esther, where His name is not mentioned, but His presence is clearly seen and felt by those who have eyes to see. We see this repeating in our day.

In our adventure of *Decoding the Prophet Jeremiah*, you will discover many crazy anomalies. For instance, the first verse of Jeremiah 25 took place in the fourth year of Jehoiakim, but the first verse of Jeremiah 45 also occurred in the fourth year of Jehoiakim. Yet, in between these chapters in the first verse of chapter 28, it was the fourth year of Zedekiah, which was eleven years later! This makes it obvious the chapters are not in order but patched together.

Decoding is also necessary when it comes to correctly translating this book. We find that the name of one of the kings of Judah, Jehoiakim, was intentionally mistranslated in Jeremiah 27:1 in some versions of the Bible with the name of another king of Judah, Zedekiah. This happened just because the translators thought there had to be a historical mistake. We will also decode other puzzles concerning the kings of Judah during the life of Jeremiah, such as some versions of 2 Chronicles 36:9 stating that Jehoiachin was eight years old when he began his reign but 2 Kings 24:8 stating he was eighteen years old when he began to reign. Is there an error in the Scriptures? Another conundrum!

We will also take an inside look at some of the family feuds and infighting taking place among the kings of Judah's descendants as they all vie for the throne. To get the full picture of why Jerusalem and the temple were destroyed, we need to start with a historical backdrop of just what led up to the tragic times of Jeremiah by briefly looking at the environment of the previous kings of Judah as well as the ones during Israel's downfall.

Some chapters of Jeremiah's book have a specific time frame, such as the "fourth year of Jehoiakim," while others must be placed during the reign of a certain king by reading the context clues within them. Finally the placement of some chapters is just plain arbitrary, in my opinion.

I've written this book as a guide to help you read the Book of Jeremiah so the book will make much more sense. I arranged the chapters during the reigns of various kings, but I realize they could be arranged differently. I did it this way because this is the chapter order in which I would recommend reading the Book of Jeremiah. I also suggest that these chapters probably took place during the rule of each king. I believe this will be a much more historically accurate order of the different chapters of Jeremiah and the order that they should be read.

By reading Jeremiah in this chapter order, you will have a better sense of what was going on. You will also see undeniable patterns that repeat in the Book of Revelation as they refer back to the prophecies found in Jeremiah! I will comment on and para-phrase the verses, bringing out the key thoughts I would like to highlight. I suggest you have your Bible open and at your side as we cover each chapter because we will be going chronologically through the chapters of Jeremiah in the following order:

Reign of King Josiah: 1, 3, 14, 17, 11, 12, 9, 15, 16, 7, 18, 19, 2

Reign of King Jehoiakim: 26, 27a, 25, 22, 45, 36, 13, 35, 4, 5, 6, 8, 10, 23

Reign of King Zedekiah: 30, 31, 24, 29, 46, 47, 48, 49,
50, 51, 27b, 28, 21, 20, 37, 34, 33, 38, 32, 39, 40, 41,
42, 43, 44, 52

I know of only one other book that tries to correctly rearrange the chapters of Jeremiah: *Jeremiah: The Fate of a Prophet* by an Israeli Jewish scholar named Binyamin Lau. For the most part, we have similarities in our groupings of chapters, with a few exceptions. There are seven chapters within the Book of Jeremiah that he doesn't include in his book: chapters 9, 12, 16, 47, 48, 50, and 51. I am not sure why he did not cover those chapters in depth, but he does quote from chapters 9 and 16. From what I read of his book, I gleaned some wonderful insights. I found one of his comments highly interesting, so I'll paraphrase it here: throughout biblical history all the prophets failed repeatedly in penetrating the collective consciousness of the people in getting them to repent. The only prophet who succeeded was Jonah, who went to the Gentiles in Nineveh.[6]

We'll also explore the fact that quite often we find insights seen in the Hebrew language that are hidden in the English language. These insights can be found in the Book of Lamentations, which most scholars believe was also written by Jeremiah.

For instance, we will explore the fact that there are twenty-two letters in the Hebrew alphabet, and there are also twenty-two verses in the first, second, fourth, and fifth chapters of Lamentations. Unbeknownst to many, the twenty-two verses in chapters 1, 2, and 4 are written in alphabetical order like an acrostic. Each verse begins with a word whose first letter goes progressively through the Hebrew alphabet. From the Hebrew language we see the book begins with the verses of chapter one in alphabetical order. A problem starts in the second chapter and multiplies in the third chapter (which has sixty-six verses), and then by the fifth chapter it has descended into total chaos, where there is no alphabetical order. We will look closer at these details and discover why two Hebrew letters are in reverse order at the end.

Fortunately we see from the text that God is in total control, even in the midst of the chaos. This gives great hope to the believer, as Yeshua also declared that He had told us in advance all the things that are coming upon our generation so we might keep our confidence, holding fast to Him in the midst of the storms of life.

I have also included timeline charts that will help you put all the pieces together. Connecting the words of other prophets who were prophesying before, during, and after Jeremiah will give you an overall view of what God was imploring His people to grasp during that epic time in history—and what He is speaking to our generation as well. I will tie together what the Books of Daniel, Ezekiel, and Esther also tell us for a better picture of what was happening. We will get a feel for the lives of the different kings of Israel and try to see from their perspective and that of their wives, getting their view of what was transpiring.

Jeremiah was known as the weeping prophet. As we read the Book of Lamentations, we see Jeremiah's profound grief over the destruction of Jerusalem, the temple, and the people themselves, who in their pride and rebellion turned from the God of Israel. Jeremiah was an incredible man because the tears he shed were not so much for himself but for God and God's people, in spite of how they treated him. These tears were not ones of self pity, even though he had every right to feel that way.

In looking at Jeremiah's background, we find he was from a family of priests, being a direct descendant of Aaron. As such, he fulfilled the roles of both a priest and a prophet. Incredibly, many of his associates wanted to kill him right along with everyone else! We find in the twenty-sixth chapter that when Jeremiah had finished speaking, everyone told him he was a dead man![7]

How well did he get along with the politicians? In chapter 38 the princes told the king to kill him![8]

Maybe his neighbors in the town of Anathoth would support him? We find in chapter 11 they were seeking to kill him as well if he continued prophesying in the name of the Lord.[9]

Hopefully he had some close friends he could rely on? Not so. In chapter 20 we find his close friends were all denouncing him, hoping he would fall and be deceived so they could overcome him and get revenge.[10]

Well, it's a good thing he at least had family, right? God revealed to him in chapter 12 that even the house of his father dealt treacherously with him, calling on a multitude to come after him and stabbing him the back while speaking sweet words to him.[11]

Maybe he at least had a wife who would be on his side? In Jeremiah 16 we find the Lord told him, "No wife for you!"[12]

He was definitely a man of sorrows, acquainted with grief and all alone. He even shared with us a few comments about what he thought of the day he was born.

> Cursed be the day wherein I was born: let not the day wherein my mother bare me be blessed. Cursed be the man who brought tidings to my father, saying, A man child is born unto thee; making him very glad. And let that man be as the cities which the LORD overthrew, and repented not: and let him hear the cry in the morning, and the shouting at noontide; because he slew me not from the womb; or that my mother might have been my grave, and her womb to be always great with me. Wherefore came I forth out of the womb to see labour and sorrow, that my days should be consumed with shame?
>
> —JEREMIAH 20:14–18

So let's jump into rediscovering this incredible priest and prophet of God by looking at what he penned as directed by the hand of God during his lifetime. What had he said that made him so alone? Wasn't he only trying to help?

One of the greatest things we can do in life is to keep a record of what the Lord is revealing to us. He loves to work through repeated patterns to help us better understand what He is trying to get through to us. With that in mind, at the end of each chapter I ask the same two questions: "What is the Lord telling you about Himself?" and "What else has the Lord taught you?" Too often we only look at what is being revealed to us for our own sakes. I want you to understand more deeply what the Scriptures are revealing about the nature and character of the Lord!

Also, by writing this book, I am trying to help you go deeper in your study of the Bible by creating a proper timeline of events. I want you to see the importance of correlating the other books of the Bible that speak about events from the same time period for a complete understanding that fills in missing information. Buckle up as we get ready to go on the adventure of a lifetime, decoding the prophet Jeremiah!

CHAPTER 1

KINGS AHAZ, HEZEKIAH, MANASSEH, AND AMON

SETTING THE STAGE—THE HISTORICAL BACKDROP

T O PROPERLY UNDERSTAND the man behind the Book of Jeremiah, we need to look at the epic events and environment during the time in which he lived, leading up to the destruction of the temple. When Jeremiah was probably around ten years old, Josiah became the king of Judah at age eight. In essence, they grew up together, being close in age.

We also need to explore what transpired during the times of Josiah's ancestors to give us a better idea of what led up to the fall of Israel's society and God's judgment upon them. We will start with King Ahaz, then follow the events with his son,

Hezekiah, and then go on to Hezekiah's son, Manasseh, and then the short reign of Josiah's father, Amon. Here's a timeline you might find helpful as you read through the lives of these kings in this chapter.

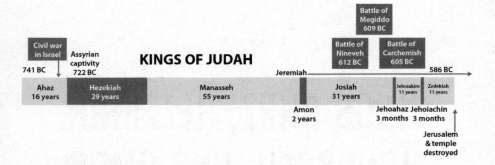

So let's get started by looking at Josiah's great-great-grandpa King Ahaz and seeing what unfolded.

King Ahaz Reigns Sixteen Years

Around 741 BC twenty-year-old Ahaz became the king of Judah and ruled for sixteen years.[1] Ahaz was the son of King Jotham and the father of Hezekiah. The kingdom of Israel was divided at this time. In the southern kingdom of Judah the royal succession went to the sons of the king. In the northern kingdom of Israel royal succession sometimes went to a son, but other times it was acquired by treachery.

Such was the case during the time of Ahaz. In the northern kingdom the Israelite king Pekahiah had reigned two years when he was assassinated by Pekah; Pekah reigned twenty years until he was murdered by Hoshea; Hoshea reigned nine years until the northern kingdom was exiled by the Assyrian king Shalmaneser in 722 BC.[2]

At the beginning of Ahaz's reign over Judah, Tiglathpileser was the king of Assyria, followed by Shalmaneser, who ruled Assyria during the last four years of Ahaz's reign. King Ahaz's son, Hezekiah, faced two kings of Assyria: Shalmaneser and then Sennacherib, who was followed by Esarhaddon.[3]

Politics and treachery went hand in hand, leading to a civil war between the two kingdoms, Israel and Judah. Following this internal conflict, an external war led to the exile of the northern tribes into Assyria.

During this time, several godly prophets were trying to get the people of God to mend their ways and to stop the baseless hatred toward each other. God's most significant challenges are never with the heathen but with His own children. Some of the greatest prophets—Isaiah, Micah, and Hosea—were trying to have an impact on Israel during this time.

Hosea proclaimed the dismal moral character of those living in the land of Israel during his day. He declared that God had a controversy with His own people. He stated that there was no truth, no mercy, and even no knowledge of God in the land. They were swearing, lying, murdering each other, and committing adultery.[4] The priests who were supposed to be teaching the people God's laws had forgotten them, and the people were being destroyed due to the lack of knowledge of the Torah, the consequence being that God would therefore forget their children![5]

The prophet Micah warned Israel over a century in advance that Jerusalem would be plowed as a field and would become heaps of ruin.[6] Many years later certain of the elders of Israel quoted Micah when Jeremiah was facing death at the hands of the other priests and prophets who had presented his words to the princes and to the people. They declared that Micah was spared around eighty years earlier, so maybe Jeremiah should be spared as well.[7]

During this time, the prophet Isaiah declared woes and warnings to God's children because they had reached the point where they were calling evil good and good evil. (Sounds like our times today.) They also considered themselves to be wise, but as the Bible says, it was only in their own eyes.[8] Just as Micah had prophesied, Isaiah also proclaimed judgment was racing toward Israel because they despised the word of the Lord, the Holy One of Israel, and cast the Law, or the Torah, of the Lord aside.[9] Many today proclaim to be wise and cast aside the Torah, throwing it into the trash bin of history.

Isaiah was the chief prophet during the time of both Ahaz and his son, Hezekiah. In the first chapter of Isaiah's prophetic utterances we hear God declaring that He had brought up children who had rebelled against Him. While animals are smart enough to know their owners, follow their instruction, and know where home is, God's own children didn't even consider they had One they were accountable to.[10]

Isaiah prophesied during the days of King Ahaz and the civil war that took place between Israel and Judah. The tribes in northern Israel were under the head of Ephraim, and those in southern Israel were led by the tribe of Judah. The king of Israel was teaming up with the king of Syria to go to war against Ahaz, the king of Judah.

Isaiah addressed King Ahaz's fears concerning the civil war, telling him to sit still because God had everything under control. Isaiah also said that within sixty-five years the northern tribes under Ephraim would no longer even be considered a people as the king of Assyria would bring destruction to both Syria and the northern tribes.[11]

Isaiah asked Ahaz if he would like a sign that this prophecy was true, but Ahaz refused. Therefore Isaiah gave Ahaz the famous prophecy that a virgin would conceive, bear a son, and call him

Immanuel. He also warned Ahaz that the king of Assyria was coming.[12]

Now comes an interesting part of the story. There is a man named Zechariah who has a daughter named Abijah, and she marries King Ahaz, becoming the mother of Hezekiah.[13]

But let's take a closer look at something absolutely incredible in the life of King Ahaz, who, as I mentioned, was only twenty years old when he began to reign. Ahaz made molten images for the Baalim. He burnt incense in the Hinnom Valley, or Valley of Blood, burning his own children in the fire, following all the abominations of the previous inhabitants.

Because Ahaz sacrificed and burned incense in every place imaginable instead of listening to God's instruction to sit still and wait for victory, the king of Syria came to Judah and took away many captives to Damascus. Ahaz, the king of Judah, was also delivered into the hands of the king of Israel, who slew one hundred twenty thousand valiant men of Judah in one day because they had forsaken the Lord. After killing one of Ahaz's sons, the children of Israel then captured two hundred thousand men, women, and children, taking them and other spoils back to Samaria.[14]

Can you imagine being married to this guy for twenty years? It would have been challenging to say the least—especially if you were a holy, righteous woman as Abijah was. Imagine your husband sacrificing your firstborn to Molech! In spite of holy prophets and people around him, the king of Judah rejected the Lord, worshipped idols, sacrificed his children, destroyed the vessels of the temple, and brought destruction upon his people.

The children of Israel began to fear that they had overdone it this time, so they sent the captives back to Judah to avoid the wrath of God. But for King Ahaz it was not over. The Edomites joined the fight and came against him along with the Philistines.[15]

Isaiah had told him to just let God do what He was doing and sit back because the king of Assyria was going to solve his problems. But, oh no, in the midst of all these attacks, Ahaz now wanted to "help" God by sending emissaries to the king of Assyria to come and help deliver him from the king of Syria and the king of Israel. So King Ahaz sent messengers to Tiglathpileser, the king of Assyria, stating that he was his servant as well as his son![16]

I can't help but be reminded of God's heartbreak in the first chapter of Isaiah, where God said at that very time His children didn't even realize He is their Father! I know today there are many believing parents whose children get led astray by people with bad intentions who try to become their surrogate parents, and the true parents yearn for their children to return. If this is you, rest assured that God knows your heartache and you can bring your burden for your children to Him.

King Ahaz gathered up all the silver and gold he could find in his own treasury as well as the temple and sent it as a present to the king of Assyria, Tiglathpileser, who then went to Damascus and destroyed the city, killing the king and taking the people captive. King Ahaz was thrilled and ran to Damascus to greet the king of Assyria. While there, Ahaz saw a really cool altar and requested one of the priests to make one just like it for him. When he returned from Damascus, he replaced God's altar with the new one and began having all the daily sacrifices on it.

In the fourth year of Ahaz's rule over Judah, Pekah, the king of Israel, was murdered by Hoshea, who later took over as king during Ahaz's twelfth year. In Hoshea's ninth year Shalmaneser, king of Assyria, conquered Samaria and took the children of Israel into captivity in what is known as the Assyrian Captivity; the northern tribes were carried away never to return again.[17]

After Ahaz died, his son, Hezekiah, began to reign at twenty-five years old. At least in Abijah he had a righteous mother. If you remember, his dad, King Ahaz, was twenty years old when he began to reign, and he reigned sixteen years, so he died at the age of thirty-six. If Hezekiah began his reign at twenty-five years old, then Hezekiah was born when his dad was about eleven years old! That also would make Hezekiah nine or ten years old when his father took the throne.

So it was during his teenage years he witnessed with his own eyes all the corruption, the devastating civil war, and the heart-break of his mother as his dad, the king of Judah, led God's people astray. Yet he also had the words of the prophets Isaiah, Hosea, and Micah echoing in his ears. So let's take a look at how all of this affected his childhood and how Hezekiah responded when it became his turn on the throne.

King Hezekiah Reigns Twenty-Nine Years

We find that Hezekiah was twenty-five years old when he became king, and he reigned twenty-nine years, dying at the age of fifty-four.[18]

King Hezekiah immediately began to restore the nation after its brutal civil war. He wrote letters to Ephraim and Manasseh, desiring that they and all Judah and Israel come to Jerusalem to keep the Passover.

Due to a lack of preparation, the priests, not having fully sanc-tified themselves as prescribed according to the Torah, were not able to keep the Passover in the first month, so they had to do it in the second month. As expected, the northern tribes laughed them to scorn and mocked them. Yet there is always a rem-nant, and some of the people from the Northern tribes made the journey to try and heal the divisions.[19]

Hezekiah had a heart after God and removed the high places, broke down all the images, and destroyed the brazen serpent that Moses had made eight hundred years earlier![20] What did

Hezekiah hear and see from the prophets who were during his reign?

- Hosea married a harlot because the people of Israel had committed great harlotry in departing from the Lord.[21]

- Hosea spoke the word of the Lord that He had written the great things of His Law, or Torah, but God's own people thought of the Torah as some strange thing.[22]

- God was telling His people to repent and to break up their fallow ground, for it was the time to seek the Lord so He could rain righteousness upon them.[23]

It is incredible to me that righteous people have no problem walking in the ways of the Lord, whereas transgressors stumble in them.[24] So many believers today stumble over God's laws, not realizing they are the right way to go.

So what did Hezekiah do? He cleaved to the Lord and kept all the commandments the Lord had commanded Moses to tell Israel eight hundred years earlier. He then rebelled against Shalmaneser, the king of Assyria. Here's an overview of the next few years:

- In Hezekiah's fourth year—which was also the seventh year of King Hoshea of Israel—the king of Assyria besieged Samaria.

- In Hezekiah's sixth year—which was also the ninth year of Hoshea—the great Assyrian Captivity took place. King Hoshea and Israel's northern tribes were taken captive because they would not obey the commandments God gave to Moses for them to keep.

- In Hezekiah's fourteenth year, the next king of Assyria, Sennacherib, came against him.[25]

The problem happened when the "like father, like son" principle came into effect: Hezekiah said he was sorry for offending the king of Assyria and submitted himself to Sennacherib. Also like his father, Hezekiah then gave the Assyrian king silver and gold from the king's treasuries and even cut off the gold from the temple doors and gave it to him.[26]

The gestures didn't help. King Sennacherib attacked anyway. So Hezekiah took counsel with his princes and mighty men of valor and came up with a battle plan. He told the citizens of Jerusalem to be strong and courageous, just as the Lord told Joshua when the people were entering the Promised Land.[27] Hezekiah told the people that the Lord was with them to fight their battles.[28]

Sennacherib sent servants to Jerusalem to harass the Jewish people. These foreign ambassadors sent by Sennacherib cried out with a loud voice in Hebrew and told the Jews to surrender. (These were more than likely some of the remnants of the northern tribes who had sided with Assyria. Rabshakeh, whose name means chief cupbearer, may very well have been Jewish.) Isaiah stood next to Hezekiah, and both men prayed and cried out to heaven for help.[29]

Let's now go to 2 Kings to fill in some of the gaps. What unfolded is just incredible! Rabshakeh warned Judah that if they trusted Egypt to help them, they were out of luck. Then in the Hebrew language, he declared that if they trusted in the Lord, it wouldn't help either because the Lord was the One who told them to come and destroy Jerusalem![30]

The Jewish people on the walls of Jerusalem could hear and understand what was being said. The Jewish rulers did not want the common people to be frightened by what he was saying, so Hezekiah's servants told Rabshakeh to quit speaking in Hebrew and instead speak in the Syrian language. That way, the rulers would understand, but the common people would not.

So Rabshakeh knew he had hit a nerve and yelled out even louder in the Hebrew language to come out and be spared. Then amazingly he quoted the words of the prophet Micah! Micah had declared that the Lord would decide disputes for strong nations far away and that nations would not fight against nations or learn war anymore. Every man will be under his vine and under his fig tree.[31] This is what Rabshakeh said to them.[32]

The servants became nervous and ran to Isaiah, who told them not to be afraid because the word from the Lord was that the king of Assyria would return to his own land, and he would die there.[33]

Now, I have to bring to your remembrance that this is happening in the fourteenth year of the twenty-nine-year reign of King Hezekiah. This is right at the midpoint. He has fifteen years to go. Here Hezekiah was facing death at the hands of the Assyrian army, and at the same time, Isaiah came to him and told him to get his house in order because he was about to die! It was then he cried out to God, and God gave him the next fifteen years.[34] It was at a time of tremendous physical attack that he experienced a tremendous spiritual attack.

Unlike his father, who refused a sign, King Hezekiah asked for a sign, and Isaiah told him the shadow of the sundial would go backward ten degrees. When you look at this carefully, you find that during the night—some Jewish sites say at midnight—the Assyrians were destroyed just like the Egyptians.[35] It is taught that this event happened on Passover! We also find that on the third day of Passover Hezekiah rose from his appointed time of death.[36]

Now let's jump back to Chronicles and see what else transpires! We find everyone was impressed with Hezekiah's amazing victory over Assyria. Hezekiah was being magnified by everyone and even all the nations around him.[37]

But when you read on, you will sadly find that it states that Hezekiah did not render to God the benefit done to him because his heart got lifted up! It says that therefore the wrath of God came upon him and Jerusalem! Then it goes on to say that Hezekiah had very great riches and honor, along with all kinds of goods and storehouses for the harvest and all types of livestock. God blessed him tremendously and gave him a lot of property.[38]

The problem is God pours out blessings upon us to test us to see if we will turn from Him. God's blessings can quickly become curses if we think we deserve them or that it was by our hand we acquired them. This is why we find that when the ambassadors from Babylon came to Hezekiah, God left him! God left him to try him that He might know all that was in Hezekiah's heart![39]

As a matter of fact we find Isaiah informing us that Merodachbaladan, the king of Babylon's son, sent letters and a present to King Hezekiah, for he had heard that Hezekiah had been sick and recovered. Hezekiah received the Babylon contingency and showed them everything he had. There was nothing he didn't show them.[40]

Therefore Isaiah told Hezekiah that everything in his house and everything he had inherited would be carried away to Babylon. Then he told Hezekiah that the sons he was yet to have would also be taken to Babylon and become eunuchs. Unbelievably, Hezekiah's response was that the word of the Lord was great as far as he was concerned because at least he would have peace and truth in his day![41]

We now move on to Hezekiah's son, Manasseh. We find Manasseh was twelve years old when he began to reign, and he reigned fifty-five years.[42]

MANASSEH REIGNS FIFTY-FIVE YEARS

Since Manasseh was twelve years old when he began to reign, that would mean he was a miracle baby who was born during Hezekiah's fifteen-year life extension. There would have been no heir to the throne of David otherwise. It seems that Manasseh grew up with a silver spoon in his mouth during the time Hezekiah was being blessed abundantly. Sadly his father was not giving God the glory for what he had obtained. Manasseh heard all the stories of the Assyrian battles and the great deliverances. Solomon's Temple was his playground. Manasseh, at twelve years old, was a bar mitzvah boy becoming accountable before God as he became king.

What did he hear from Isaiah, Hosea, and Micah? Micah declared that in the last days Jerusalem would be the capital of the world, all nations would come to Jerusalem as the God of Israel taught them the Torah and taught them His ways, all would walk in His paths, and the word of the Lord and His Torah would spread out from Jerusalem![43]

But Micah also declared that the Lord had a controversy with His own people. He pleaded with Manasseh's nation, asking what He had done to weary them and asking them to testify against Him so He would know their accusations.[44] We discover that the nation had grown tired of serving God, believing it was a burden to do all He had required of them. They responded to God by asking if it would even make Him happy if they brought thousands of rams or ten thousand rivers of oil. Then they really slapped God in the face by saying maybe He would be pleased if they sacrificed their firstborn for their transgressions.[45]

Micah responds that the Lord had shown them what He requires of them, and it was simply to do justly, love mercy, and to walk humbly with your God.[46] I don't know about you, but when I read this, something really jumps out to me. It doesn't say to walk humbly in front of this all-powerful and prideful God, but we are to walk with a humble God! I stand aghast as I think of people in all their pride, standing beside a humble God who has real power and authority and is able to move mountains with a single word. People are so foolish.

Then Manasseh heard the words of Hosea telling Israel to return to God as they have fallen by their iniquity.[47] What was his response?

We find he rebuilt all the pagan altars his father, Hezekiah, had taken down. He rebuilt the high places, raised up altars for Baalim, made groves, and even built altars to worship all the host of heaven in the two courts of the house of the Lord! He also sacrificed his own children to Molech, consulted with familiar spirits and wizards, used witchcraft, and set a carved image he personally built in the house of God.[48] According to Jewish tradition, he set it up on the seventeenth day of Tammuz, the very same date that Moses broke the first tablets inscribed with the Ten Commandments upon seeing that the Israelites had worshipped the golden calf.[49] Unbelievable! A teenage brat became king.

How would you like to be a single mother raising this child, watching him sacrifice your grandchildren to Molech? So just who was Manasseh's mother, the wife of Hezekiah? Was she righteous or wicked?

Isaiah prophesied that one day Jerusalem would no longer be called Forsaken, but she would be called *Hephzibah* (my delight is in her); the land would be called Beulah, for the Lord delights in her; and the Land would be married.[50] Then come the famous verses about how the Lord had set up watchmen on the walls of Jerusalem who will never hold their peace until He makes Jerusalem a praise in the earth.[51]

Believe it or not, Jewish history records that Hephzibah was the daughter of Isaiah.[52] She married Hezekiah, and she was also the mother of Manasseh![53] That would make Isaiah and Hezekiah in-laws! Isaiah had been rebuking Hezekiah, his son-in-law, and now he had to deal with Israel's most wicked king, Manasseh—his own grandson! And who was Hephzibah going to side with: her son, who was murdering her own grandchildren, or her father, Isaiah? Imagine how Grandpa Isaiah felt with a wicked grandson who threw his own great-grandchildren into the fires of Molech.

Let me tell you a little bit of Jewish history. In the Book of Hebrews chapter 11, the faith chapter, it talks about those who were stoned, sawn asunder, tempted, slain with the sword, and so on.[54] If you research this, you will find that according to Jewish historical writings, Isaiah was the one who was sawn asunder. Not only that, he was sawn asunder by his own grandson, Manasseh, as he was hiding from him in a tree![55]

God had had enough. He declared by His servants the prophets that because of all King Manasseh had done, He was going to bring such evil on Jerusalem and Judah that the ears of all who heard of it would tingle. He declared that He would wipe out Jerusalem, turning it upside down and delivering its people into their enemies' hands. Manasseh had shed innocent blood until he had filled Jerusalem from one end to the other.[56]

God spoke directly to Manasseh and the people, but they refused to listen. As a result God brought the captain of the army of Assyria, who took Manasseh among the thorns, bound him with fetters, and hauled him off to Babylon.[57]

Then another unlikely event happened. Manasseh greatly humbled himself before God and earnestly prayed, and God heard his prayer! God restored him to the kingdom, and Manasseh took away all the strange gods and the idol he built from of the house of the Lord, and he cast all the idols out of the city. He then repaired the altar of the Lord and made sacrifices, peace offerings, and thanksgiving offerings. He commanded Judah to serve the Lord God of Israel.[58] Unbelievable! Then came his son, Amon.

AMON REIGNS TWO YEARS

Amon was twenty-two when he ascended to the throne, and he reigned only two years before he was assassinated by his own servants in his own house! He also did evil in the sight of the Lord, sacrificing to all the carved images and refusing to humble himself. The people of the land then slew those who had killed Amon and installed his son, Josiah, as king.[59] Amon died at twenty-four years old, and Josiah was eight when he became king, meaning he was born when his dad was only sixteen years old.[60] Imagine being an eight-year-old when your dad is murdered in your own house!

Let's summarize some thoughts.

The Bible clearly shows how dysfunctional all of humanity is, even God's own kids, past and present included. We see civil war breaking out among God's people—children against parents and grandparents, and parents killing their own children. There truly is nothing new under the sun. We also wonder about God's fairness when He seems to acquit the wicked and hold the righteous accountable. Over and over we see a pattern of what happens when God's laws are disregarded. We also more clearly understand how our rebellion affects God's heart. God always warns before He brings judgment, and if we would only repent, life would be so different.

QUESTIONS

- What is the Lord telling you about Himself?

- What else has the Lord taught you?

CHAPTER 2

JOSIAH: THE BOY KING

JEREMIAH 1

T HIS BRINGS US to King Josiah, who was the king of Judah during the life and times of Jeremiah. Imagine being anointed king at eight years old. We're talking about a second grader! The prophet Jeremiah grew up with him, being only around two years older. You know Josiah had to have many tutors speaking into his life. The righteous were no doubt instructing him about the word of the Lord, as expressed through the prophets. And one prophecy, in particular, would have stood out.

It was given around three hundred years earlier when King Jeroboam decided he could determine when the feasts of the Lord should be kept and decided to build altars in Bethel and Dan to worship golden calves at these locations. These were dates he devised in his own heart because he was worried that Israel would continue to worship in Jerusalem after the kingdom was divided between him and Rehoboam.[1]

After this happened, a man of God came out of Judah and spoke to Jeroboam in Bethel as he was burning incense. He cried out, stating a child would be born to the house of David—Josiah by name—and that upon that altar he would offer the priests of the high places that were burning incense on it.[2] Can you imagine what Josiah thought when this three-hundred-year-old prophecy was read to him?

We find Josiah reigned for a total of thirty-one-years, dying at the age of thirty-nine. In the eighth year of his reign, when he was sixteen years old, he began to seek after the God of David his father. At that time, he had one child and his wife was pregnant with another. Then in his twelfth year as king, at the age of twenty, he began to purge Judah and Jerusalem from all the high places, the Asherim, and all the molten images.[3] A year later, when Josiah was twenty-one, in the thirteenth year of his reign, his oldest son, Jehoiakim, was seven years old. Jeremiah was around twenty-three, and the prophecies of Jeremiah began! Open your Bible, if you so desire, and read chapter one of Jeremiah.

God Speaks to Jeremiah

We see Jeremiah was the son of Hilkiah, one of the priests who lived in Anathoth, just north of Jerusalem in the land of Benjamin. It was in the thirteenth year of Josiah that the word of the Lord came to Jeremiah.[4] In the twenty-first chapter of Joshua we find God was designating certain cities in the Promised Land to be reserved for the priests. One of those cities was Anathoth.[5] The word of the Lord came to Jeremiah, informing him that not only had God preplanned Josiah, but He knew Jeremiah before he was even formed in the womb. God had sanctified him before he was born and ordained him to be a prophet not just to Israel but the nations as well.[6]

Much like what happened with Moses, Jeremiah proclaimed that he couldn't speak well because he was just a kid. God told him it didn't matter and that he was simply to speak whatever he was commanded and not to be afraid. So God touched Jeremiah's mouth and told him that He would place His words in his mouth.[7] To Jeremiah's amazement, God promoted him and declared that he was now over nations and kingdoms, and his job was to "root out, and to pull down, and to destroy, and to throw down, to build, and to plant."[8] We know from the Scriptures that everything has its season. There is a time to pluck and a time to plant, and God was telling Jeremiah it was plucking time, as Nebuchadnezzar was about to overturn many nations.

God spoke again to Jeremiah, asking him what he was seeing, and he saw a rod of an almond tree. The Lord confirmed he was correct, declaring that He was watching over His word to perform it.[9] Unless you know Hebrew, you miss the play on words. The Hebrew word for *almond*, שָׁקֵד, is spelled the same as the word for *watching over*. But the difference is in how it sounds. The first time it is "shaw-ked" and the second time it is "show-ked." God always keeps His word and even exalts it to a higher place than His name.

Then the word of the Lord came a second time to Jeremiah, asking him what he saw, and Jeremiah described a seething pot facing the north. The Lord told Jeremiah that from the north, evil was coming upon all the inhabitants of the land of Israel.[10]

Oh great! Who wants to be the bearer of bad news? God said that He makes sure His word is performed, and the word at that time was that judgment was coming upon the nation of Israel. God told Jeremiah to man up and get prepared. He was not to be afraid even though all of Israel—from the kings and priests to the common people of the land—were fighting against him. He was told not to be afraid because God Himself would be there right along with him, defending him.[11] God gave Jeremiah plenty of time to prepare—from the thirteenth to the eighteenth year of Josiah's reign, when the king finally purged the land of all idolatry and sent his servants to repair the house of the Lord. Josiah was twenty-six years old,[12] and the prophet/priest Jeremiah was about twenty-eight.

By this time, the northern tribes had wholeheartedly joined in the financing of the rebuilding of the temple, along with those from Judah and Benjamin, and many had returned to Jerusalem. They all joined in the work of repairing what "the kings of Judah had destroyed."[13]

We find Hilkiah was the high priest at this time.[14] I can't help but wonder if this Hilkiah was Jeremiah's father. Incredibly Hilkiah found the Book of the Law of the Lord and had it read before King Josiah, who tore his clothes, declaring that God's wrath would be coming upon them all for the disobedience of his fathers.[15]

I want to point out at this time that Josiah's son Jehoiakim was now at bar mitzvah age, the age of accountability, when he lived through these historical events. It's easy to imagine that he saw his father, Josiah, tearing his clothes in fear and grief as he heard that the coming wrath of God would be great.

Josiah ordered they consult the Lord about this, so they went to Huldah the prophetess, who prophesied that because Josiah humbled himself when he heard of God's coming judgment, he would be spared ever seeing the disaster and go to his grave in peace.[16] Wait a minute, Huldah! I can just see Josiah being caught between a rock and a hard place. He just heard about God destroying the place because of idols, and he is about to devote his life to tearing down the idols. It was as if she was telling him all his efforts would be in vain. Josiah went on the warpath to prove Huldah wrong. Why wasn't Jeremiah consulted? Where did he stand on this issue?

In this eighteenth year of his reign Josiah brought out of the house of the Lord all the vessels made for Baal and for the host of heaven, as well as those made for the Asherah shrine. He burned them in the Kidron Valley and carried the ashes to Bethel. He then put down all the idolatrous priests, whom the kings of Judah had ordained to burn incense in all the high places around Jerusalem.[17]

You will absolutely not believe what came next! Guess what was sitting right next to the house of the Lord? The Bible goes on to say that Josiah then broke down the houses of the sodomites that were by the house of the Lord, where the women wove hangings for the shrine of Asherah![18]

Then King Josiah defiled Tophet, which is in the Hinnom Valley.[19] The Hebrew word *toph* refers to a hand drum, and some biblical scholars have speculated that the place name Topeth is derived from it because people would loudly beat on drums to drown out the cries of the children as they were being thrown into the fire on the altars of Molech.

Josiah took away the horses that the kings of Judah had given to the sun at the entrance to the house of the Lord! He also demolished the altars his grandfather Manasseh made that had somehow reappeared in the two courts of the house of the Lord.[20]

Now comes, in my opinion, one of the most shocking events in the whole Bible. It has to do with the Mount of Olives, which at this time—over four hundred years after King Solomon's reign—had become so defiled it was known as the Mount of Corruption. We find that King Josiah destroyed all the high places south of the Mount of Corruption, which Solomon had built for Ashtoreth, the abomination of the Zidonians; for Chemosh, the abomination of the Moabites; and for Milcom, the abomination of the Ammonites, breaking in pieces the images and cutting down the groves.[21]

To me this is so incredible! Solomon was the first Israelite king to allow child sacrifice, offering up his own child on the altar to Molech! We can assume this because among his hundreds of wives were an Ammonite and a Moabite for whom he built altars, allowing them to make sacrifices.[22] Solomon was the one who promoted all the pagan sacrifices and built over a thousand pagan altars all around Jerusalem! Israel figured if it was good enough for wise old Solomon, surely it is good enough for them! The Torah clearly stated that anyone who worshipped Ashtoreth or offered children to Molech was to be stoned. If anyone turned a blind eye to the worship of Molech, then judgment would fall on that person as well.[23]

It seems eerily just like today where just as there are banks too big to fail and politicians too big to hold accountable, no one wanted to hold King Solomon responsible, and the repercussions resonated throughout the centuries, leading to the eventual destruction of Solomon's Temple. I go much more into detail of Solomon's horrific evil and the turning of his back on God in my book *Decoding the Antichrist and the End Times*. Israel's moral character has remained the same. Regardless of all the blessings God has bestowed upon them, they still rebel against Him and will not do what He says!

While all this was going on, Josiah discovered that his birth and even his name were prophesied three hundred years earlier by an unnamed man of God during the reign of Jeroboam! The three-hundred-year-old prophecy also mentioned what God wanted him to do with the pagan altars Jeroboam had built.[24] Josiah then went to Bethel and broke down the altar Jeroboam built, burned the high place, and burned down the groves. He saw the sepulchers and, as the prophecy stated, he took the bones and burned them on the altar.[25]

In this eighteenth year Josiah held the greatest Passover in all of Israel's history.[26] Also at this time, Josiah decided to call the nation together so they could all hear the word of the Lord for their generation from the Torah even though it was spoken almost one thousand years earlier. He knew the Torah was still alive. So he read in everyone's hearing the words of the covenant, and his generation covenanted with God to walk after Him and keep His statutes and judgments with all their heart and soul to perform them.[27]

What were the words of the covenant that he read that had him so terrified? You can read them for yourself from Deuteronomy 27:11–29:1. It would bring terror into anybody's heart—particularly Deuteronomy 28:15 through the end of that chapter. In verse 37 it declares their disobedience will lead them to "become an astonishment, a proverb, and a byword" among all the nations they went to. This prophecy is referred to many times in the Book of Jeremiah. In Deuteronomy 28:49–52 Josiah heard it prophesied that a nation would come against Israel as swift as an eagle flies, and what do we find but Ezekiel declaring the word of the Lord one thousand years later:

> And the word of the LORD came unto me, saying, Son of man, put forth a riddle, and speak a parable unto the house of Israel; and say, Thus saith the Lord GOD; A great eagle with great wings, longwinged, full of feathers, which had divers colours, came unto Lebanon, and took the highest branch of the cedar.
>
> —EZEKIEL 17:1–3

Ezekiel then explained this prophecy was all about Babylon coming.

> Moreover the word of the LORD came unto me, saying, Say now to the rebellious house, Know ye not what these things mean? tell them, Behold, the king of Babylon is come to Jerusalem, and hath taken the king thereof, and the princes thereof, and led them with him to Babylon.
> —EZEKIEL 17:11–12

In Deuteronomy 28:53 God warned them that at the time of this fulfillment, they would also eat their own children due to hunger. This is exactly what God said would happen in Jeremiah 19:7–9. You can see why King Josiah was concerned! Around the same time, Nabopolassar became king of Babylon and achieved independence from Assyria. In the next chapter we will see what the prophet Zephaniah had to say.

But first let's summarize some thoughts.

It was King Solomon's rebellion that led to pagan idols being placed in the temple precincts around Jerusalem and all throughout the land of Israel. Solomon was the one who initiated child sacrifice in Israel. Solomon's life and character are what led to the demise of the nation of Israel and were the direct cause of its division. Then, three hundred years later, King Josiah had the chutzpah to finally destroy all the pagan altars. The people appeared to be repentant, and God was ready to judge. Would His warning be heeded?

QUESTIONS

- What is the Lord telling you about Himself?

- What else has the Lord taught you?

CHAPTER 3

PUNISHMENT BEGINS

JEREMIAH 3 AND 14

WE'VE ALREADY LEARNED that Josiah was the great-grandson of King Hezekiah, and in the first verse of Zephaniah we find out that Zephaniah was the great-great-grandson of King Hezekiah. This means Zephaniah was related to King Josiah. And it just so happens he had a word from the Lord during Josiah's day.[1]

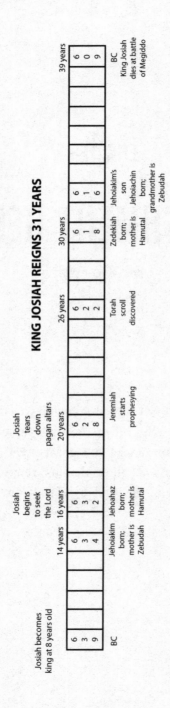

KING JOSIAH REIGNS 31 YEARS

	14 years	16 years		20 years		26 years		30 years		39 years	

Josiah becomes king at 8 years old — 639 BC

Jehoiakim born; mother is Zebudah — 634 BC

Josiah begins to seek the Lord — Jehoahaz born; mother is Hamutal — 632 BC

Josiah tears down pagan altars — Jeremiah starts prophesying — 628 BC

Torah scroll discovered — 622 BC

Zedekiah born; mother is Hamutal — 618 BC

Jehoiakim's son Jehoiachin born; grandmother is Zebudah — 616 BC

King Josiah dies at battle of Megiddo — 609 BC

Zephaniah had some strong words for King Josiah. He declared that God was going to literally wipe everything off the face of the earth and stretch His hand against Judah and all the inhabitants of Jerusalem.[2] He then encouraged a moment of silence as the day of the Lord was drawing near. No kidding! He described the day of the Lord as the Lord having prepared a sacrifice and inviting guests to come to it. Then he had the chutzpah to say God was going to punish the officials and even the king's own sons, as well as all of those who had arrayed themselves in foreign attire.[3] What was that all about?

I can't help but be reminded of a parable by Yeshua in Matthew 22. In verses 1–3 He compared the kingdom of heaven to a certain king who arranged a marriage for his son and sent his servants to call all those who were invited to the wedding, but they didn't want to come. In verses 9–12 the servants went into the highways, inviting everyone they could find, and it didn't matter if they were bad or good. When the wedding was filled, the king came out to see all the guests, and he saw one not wearing a wedding garment. The king called him a friend but had him bound hand and foot and thrown into outer darkness. This parable represents that someday all the King's kids (believers) will be invited to a wedding (the marriage supper of the Lamb), but some won't be allowed to attend because they are not wearing the wedding garment provided by the King but coming in their own finery (their own righteousness).

Many are familiar with the parable of the wise and foolish virgins, in which some attend the wedding and others do not.[4] Did you know there is a similar parable for the men? We find it in Luke 12, where the men are told to have their loins girded and to have their lamps burning. One problem though: they have already missed the wedding. But we see they still get the chance to attend the meal if they are watching this time and open the door immediately after He knocks when He returns from the wedding![5]

This also reminds me of the Song of Songs, when the bride is at the point of death and hears her beloved knocking loudly on the door, telling her to get up and open the door because his head is filled with dew and his hair with the drops of the night. In other words, it is pouring down rain![6] But he doesn't want in; he wants her to come out and experience the rain. The rain speaks of the blessings of God.[7]

But look at the bride's response! She whines that she has already taken off her raincoat. Does she really have to put it on again? She has even washed her feet, and if she goes outside, they'll just get all muddy! She hears him rattling the door handle, and she claims how much she loves him. She finally gets up, but of course she makes him wait while she gets all gussied up. Finally she puts her fingers on the handle of the lock. She unlocks the door and opens it to find he's gone! She sought him and couldn't find him; she called him, and he gave no answer! The watchmen of the city then smote her, wounded her, and took away her veil![8]

This is the problem with many in the body of Messiah today. The Lord is calling us to get out of the four walls and join Him in the harvest. In her current state the bride is not eagerly awaiting His return. She is not looking out the window, expecting Him. Not only is the door shut, but it is also locked and barred! Not only won't she go out, but she doesn't even want anyone to come in. Oh yeah, she professes to love Him, but it is all talk. This is why Jeremiah quoted the Lord, saying He will only be found when we search for Him with all our hearts.[9]

In Zephaniah we see the Lord searching Jerusalem with lamps and punishing all those who are complacent and believe that the Lord won't do good or evil. He then shouted out that the great day of the Lord was very near and coming quickly.[10] Then, as we just learned, he proclaimed that the people of Israel had better seek the Lord in humility before the Lord's anger fell and maybe they would be hidden in the day of the Lord's anger![11] I don't know about you, but I would take that warning seriously!

Then Zephaniah went on to warn the rebellious who had not obeyed God's voice but instead refused correction, didn't trust the Lord, and didn't draw near to Him. As a matter of fact he compared the princes to roaring lions and the judges to evening wolves. The prophets were called insolent and treacherous, and the priests were accused of polluting the sanctuary and doing violence to the Torah.[12]

Speaking of doing violence to the Law, some of the mega pastors today with churches in the tens of thousands claim the Hebrew Scriptures portray God as unapproachable and tell believers they need to unhitch from the Old Testament. Yet Zephaniah declared that God would restore a pure language so that all the nations may call upon the Lord together.[13] This will be a reversal of the Tower of Babel, and all the nations will again speak one language, and I believe that will be the Hebrew language. So you can either start learning Hebrew now or wait for the free heavenly download coming very soon!

Amazingly the next verses talk about God bringing His worshippers from beyond the rivers of Ethiopia, the daughter of His dispersed ones leaving in their midst a meek and humble people who will trust in the name of the Lord.[14] I can't help but think of what has been happening in just the last few years, as so many Ethiopian Jews have been migrating back to Israel.

Zephaniah then gave a word of encouragement from the Lord to King Josiah, stating that Jerusalem was not to fear because God would be in her midst and regather all those taken captive.[15] So what was Jeremiah talking about? Jeremiah had picked up on what Hosea had been prophesying a century earlier, and he was telling the people that they had played the harlot. So why were they now trying to return to the Lord, and wouldn't the land be greatly polluted if they did?[16]

GOD SENDS A DROUGHT

Israel was experiencing a significant drought, which was another curse from the covenantal agreement in Deuteronomy 28. As I mentioned, the rain was a sign of blessing from heaven. Jeremiah told them that their harlotry was the reason the rains had been withheld, because they refused to be ashamed.[17]

The word of the Lord came to Jeremiah specifically during the reign of King Josiah, asking him if he realized what backsliding Israel had done. God explained that even after they had played the harlot, God asked Israel to return to Him, but she refused. Then her treacherous sister Judah saw that she didn't fear God and went and played the harlot also. God said He wrote Israel a bill of divorce that her sister Judah witnessed.[18]

Concerning Jerusalem, we find the Bible refers to Samaria in the north as her older sister as well as Sodom in the south as being her younger sister. Both play the role of the harlot. This is why Ezekiel, who lived during the same time as Jeremiah, told Jerusalem that she was even more corrupt than they were.[19] This is why in spite of all the great reformation during the time of Josiah, God looked at the heart and said the change in Judah was all fake.

The Lord told Jeremiah that Judah had not returned with their whole heart but only in pretense; therefore Israel was more righteous because at least she was honest.[20] God wants us to be true to ourselves and Him. Be cold or hot but not a backstabber. How often do we see revival break out, such as right after 9/11, and then after as little as a few months it's right back to our old ways?

Jeremiah told the northern tribes that if they returned, God's anger would not fall on them because He was full of mercy. All He asked for was an acknowledgment that they had sinned in not obeying His voice. He claimed He was still married to them and yearning to bring them back.[21]

The drought that was hanging on was having a very grave effect. The word of the Lord came to Jeremiah, stating that the cry of Jerusalem had gone up, and everyone was looking for water but not finding it anywhere. Everyone was covering their heads, the land was parched, and there was no rain.[22] This was a direct fulfillment of the curse that they read when they reentered the covenant.

> The LORD shall make the rain of thy land powder and dust: from heaven shall it come down upon thee, until thou be destroyed.
>
> —DEUTERONOMY 28:24

What happened next is astounding, and I stand aghast. If you were Jeremiah and you were experiencing this yourself, as well as seeing all the suffering around you, what would you do? Did you say, "Pray"? Well, get a load of this! The Lord told Jeremiah not to pray for the people! He said that if even if they fasted, He wouldn't hear their cry. Even when they offered up burnt offerings, He wouldn't accept them, and He was going to consume them with the sword, famine, and pestilence![23] In other words, it's as if He were saying, "Too bad, so sad."

However, Jeremiah was fit to be tied, explaining to God that the people were being deceived by false prophets telling them they would not see the sword or famine and would only have peace. God told Jeremiah the prophets were all liars; He never sent them, commanded them, or even spoken to them. They were speaking divination out of the deceit of their hearts. As a result all of the false prophets' wives and children would be destroyed.[24]

The prophets threw God's name around to give their words a sense of authority. This reminds me of a verse in the Gospel of Matthew. It says a high number will call Him Lord, saying that they were prophets who prophesied in His name, sent out evil spirits in His name, and by His name did many wonderful works of power, but He will tell them that He never knew them and to depart as they are only workers of evil![25]

God had Jeremiah prophesy about the coming destruction, declaring His eyes were running down with tears day and night because of the breach upon Judah. If the prophet went into the field, there were the bodies of the slain by the sword; if he entered the city, there were those sick with famine. Both the prophet and the priest went about in a land they don't even know.[26] The devastation had become so bad the locals couldn't even find their way around. It would be like the aftermath of a tornado or hurricane, when you go back to retrieve things and can't find your own neighborhood because it has been so devasted.

Let's summarize some thoughts.

There are many relationships we have with the Lord. We are His children, we are His servants, and we are also described as the bride. We saw at the beginning of this chapter that God will punish His own children who try to come to Him in their own self-righteousness. We also see where the bride falls asleep and doesn't want to work with the Bridegroom in bringing in the harvest. I do not believe the whole body of the Messiah will become the bride, but only a remnant will. Just as Eve came from a part of the body of the first Adam, so the bride will come from a part of the body of the second Adam, the Messiah. As His children we have been rebellious. As His bride we have committed adultery by abandoning our covenant relationship to Him and turning to other lovers. God weeps over the broken relationship.

QUESTIONS

- What is the Lord telling you about Himself?

- What else has the Lord taught you?

CHAPTER 4

IT'S ALL TALK

JEREMIAH 17, 11, 12, AND 9

As we get ready to explore these four chapters of Jeremiah, I can't help but be reminded that God told Isaiah His own children would draw near with their mouths and honor Him with their lips but their hearts were far from Him, and their fear of Him was taught by the commandment of men.[1] Well, not much had changed a few generations later when Ezekiel was told while he was in captivity that the people thought he had a lovely voice, sang very well, and was even good on the instrument. The words to his songs were great, but the people sure wouldn't do what he was singing![2]

Judah's sin had been carved into their hearts by a pen of iron with a diamond tip. Therefore God said they had kindled a fire within Him, and He determined they would be sent into an enemy's land where they would experience firsthand what it was like to be servants to another, and all their wealth and treasures would be plundered.[3]

Jeremiah then reminded the people of the first psalm, stating the righteous will be like a tree planted by the rivers of water, but the wicked will be cursed—except he reversed the order and began with how the man who trusts in man and whose heart departs from the Lord will be cursed, reminding them of the drought conditions they were in and how they would be like shrubs in the desert, dwelling in a parched land. Then Jeremiah went into how the one who trusted the Lord would be like the tree planted by the waters, wouldn't need to be careful during drought, and would never cease from bearing fruit.[4]

The psalmist asked God to search him and to know his heart and thoughts to see if there was any wicked way in them.[5] You would think we would know our own hearts and thoughts, wouldn't you? Yet we read in Jeremiah that our hearts are very deceitful and that the Lord searches all our hearts to reward us according to the fruit of our doings.[6]

JEREMIAH 17 AND 11

We come to an amazing verse with phenomenal New Testament connections, so I want to have you read it right here before you.

> O Lord, the hope of Israel, all that forsake thee shall be ashamed, and they that depart from me shall be written in the earth, because they have forsaken the Lord, the fountain of living waters. Heal me, O Lord, and I shall be healed; save me, and I shall be saved: for thou art my praise. Behold, they say unto me, Where is the word of the Lord? let it come now.
> —Jeremiah 17:13–15

When we read the Gospel of John, in the seventh chapter, we find Yeshua had gone up to Jerusalem for the Feast of Tabernacles. On the last day of the feast Yeshua stood up and cried out that if anyone was thirsty, they could come to Him and drink, and whoever believed in Him, out of his belly would flow rivers of living water.[7] It goes on to say that the officers went to the chief priests and Pharisees and told them the reason they never arrested Him was because He spoke like no other ever did. They responded that the officers were deceived like the rest of the people and that those who do not know the Law are cursed![8] Therefore we see the chief priests and Pharisees didn't even realize they were the ones with the deceived hearts and had just forsaken the fountain of living waters.

Watch how this unfolds. In the very next chapter of John we have the story of the adulterous woman. Historically the Feast of Tabernacles is seven days long, and the last day is known as Shemini Atzeret, or the eighth day, and is to be a day of Sabbath rest. It is also known as Simchat Torah, or Rejoicing in the Torah, when they were to study God's Word and rejoice in the fact that He gave them such a wonderful Law and will one day tabernacle with them again. As a matter of fact this is what the psalmist felt over and over in Psalm 119, when he continually wrote how much he loved the Law of God.[9]

So in John 8 they were misapplying God's Law in several ways. They were supposed to be rejoicing in God's Law, but instead they abused it and tried to use it as a reason to kill someone. So they asked Yeshua what the Word of the Lord was in this matter. The woman was looking to Yeshua to save her from certain death by the hard-hearted religious leaders who had just forsaken the fountain of living waters the day before. What did He do? Yeshua stooped on the ground and began to write in the earth. When He stood up and they saw what He had written, they were all ashamed and began to depart as He stooped back down and continued writing in the earth.[10]

Now go back and read Jeremiah 17:13–15, and you will be amazed at the correlation. The same is also true in our day as many religious leaders misapply the Torah, using it as a weapon rather than the loving document it really is—much like the bottle that falls from heaven in the film *The Gods Must Be Crazy*; people are clueless and begin to use it in ways it never was intended to be used.

So the Lord told His people the importance of keeping the Sabbath because He wanted to have an entire day as a Father spending time with His children. And if they listened to Him and obeyed Him, desiring to spend time with Him, the city of Jerusalem would remain forever![11] After all, honoring the Sabbath was one of "the big ten."

Then God went on to explain that if they did not listen to Him and refused to keep the Sabbath, then He would have to burn the place down.[12] Imagine a rebellious teenager whose parents have to kick him out of the house because he is totally damaging the house, being extremely disruptive, and causing great harm. Of course the teenager is all self-absorbed and angrily departs, wondering why no one understands. He knows his mom and dad are upset, but he may be unaware of just how upset.

It's one thing to kick the child out of the house, and it's another if, on top of that, the parents also burn the house down and move! Now he really knows his parents meant business! This happened to Israel twice—and on the very same day, the ninth of Av—around 660 years apart. I know they took note! All of this happened because they did not obey Torah, or God's Law.

You know the old saying, "Fool me once, shame on you. Fool me twice, shame on me." As far as the Jews are concerned, there will never be a fool me a third time. That is why Jews are bewildered when Christians tell them the Law was done away with and now they are under a curse if they even try to obey God according to the Torah. They can't imagine that a God who punished them so severely for not obeying Him will now punish them severely if they even think of trying to obey Him or to keep the Sabbath.

The Lord told Jeremiah the words he was to proclaim in all the cities of Judah and in the streets of Jerusalem. The word from the Lord began with the curse to the one who did not hear and obey the words of this covenant. He wanted Jeremiah to explain how, from the very beginning when He brought Israel out of Egypt, He would get up early and protest to their fathers, telling them to obey His voice. They not only refused, they didn't even pay attention to Him and everyone walked after their own evil hearts. Jeremiah responded with a big amen, and God told Jeremiah to go and proclaim everywhere that the people needed to hear the words of this covenant and do them.[13] This hearkens back to when the people of Israel came out of Egypt, standing on either side of Mount Gerizim and Mount Ebal, proclaiming the words of the covenant. We find that cursed is whoever does not confirm all the words of the Law to do them, and everyone is to say amen.[14]

Then came the frightful word from the Lord to Jeremiah that He was going to bring evil upon the place; when His people cried out to Him, He would not listen, and when they cried out to their gods, they certainly wouldn't save them in their time of trouble.[15] If they wouldn't listen to God when He called, why should they expect Him to answer them when they called?

A second time God told Jeremiah that he was not even to lift up a cry or prayer for the people as there was no way He would hear them when they cried out in their trouble.[16] I cannot imagine a scarier situation than to be crying out to God and be told God will not hear you and won't even listen to those praying on your behalf!

Many of you are familiar with the verses in Romans 11:16–17 where Rabbi Shaul (the apostle Paul) speaks of branches being broken off from the olive tree due to unbelief, or actually a lack of trust in God, and consequently the Gentiles would be grafted in. It just so happens that comes directly from Jeremiah 11:16–17!

The Lord referred to Israel and Judah as a green olive tree with broken branches. Jeremiah felt he was the only living tree bearing fruit anywhere around Jerusalem. God then revealed to Jeremiah what the people really thought about him, and he became really upset! He couldn't believe how clueless he had been about their feelings, and he explained that he was like a lamb or an ox being led to the slaughter and was totally unaware of all that the people wanted to do to him. They had devised plans against him, wanting to cut him off from the land of the living so that he would no more be remembered.[17]

So Jeremiah told God, "Go get 'em for me!"[18] God assured him that He would. If you remember, Jeremiah lived in a city of priests called Anathoth. God informed Jeremiah that He had his back concerning the men of Anathoth—the ones telling him not to prophesy in the name of the Lord or he would die by their hands. God said that He would not only punish them but their sons and daughters as well, to where not even one of them would be left. And God kept His word. Some died by the sword, and their children died from famine. God even scheduled an appointed time to bring the evil upon them.[19]

Jeremiah 12 and 9

As we move on to Jeremiah chapter twelve, we find Jeremiah complained to God about His judgments. In particular Jeremiah questioned why God allowed the wicked to prosper. He told God that He was the One who planted them, and He allowed them to take root and bring forth fruit, yet they were happy even while they were dealing treacherously. Oh yeah, they talked about God, but God was far from being the one in control of their lives.[20] Jeremiah told God he had enough! Slaughter them! The land was suffering and the animals were dying, all because they believed God wasn't watching their wickedness.[21]

God basically told Jeremiah to man up, saying that if he was already worn out by running with the footmen, what would he do when he had to run against the horses? Then God broke the news to Jeremiah that even his brethren from the house of his father had dealt treacherously with him by calling a multitude of people against him. They were total backstabbers, speaking one thing to Jeremiah's face and then speaking against him behind his back.[22]

The very same thing was happening to Ezekiel in Babylon. God told Ezekiel that the people were all talking about him beside the walls and in the doors of their houses, telling everyone to come and hear the word of the Lord from Ezekiel! They all sat before him and listened to his words, but they wouldn't do anything the word of the Lord directed them to do. While they were giving him lip service with their mouths, their hearts were really after their own gain.[23]

In so many churches the pews are filled with people who come to hear the Word of the Lord and the lovely songs, yet their hearts are far from Him and are only there for personal gain. Their minds are filled with what they will do as soon as the service is over. Maybe they are there to make a sale, find a spouse, talk about the news of the day, or just keep up the appearance of being a good Christian—anything but do what the pastor says. Of course, many pastors are only bringing milk and cookies to the table, giving out one Bible verse and then becoming a life coach, forgetting the weightier matters of the Bible. The Book of James talks about how we need to become doers of the Word and not hearers only.[24]

God declared to Jeremiah how broken He was; He was forsaking His house and delivering His own children into the hands of the enemies because they were acting like lions, crying out against Him. He went on to say that it was the many shepherds, or pastors, who had destroyed His vineyard, making it desolate.[25]

Then, remarkably, the Lord declared that there will be forgiveness because He was in covenant. It's similar to people saying that they can say whatever they want against their brothers or sisters, but if you say anything, they'll whip you. While God was saying that He would cast His children into the neighboring enemy's territory, when these enemies came into possession of the land of Israel, He was going to pluck Israel and Judah back out of those lands and give them back the Promised Land. He would return and have compassion on them.[26]

Then comes an amazing statement. God declared that if those from the other nations who were in the land of Israel would only learn to swear by God's name, then just as they had taught the Jewish people to swear by their false gods, they would now be able to be built up in the midst of His people; otherwise, out they go![27]

Jeremiah was about at the end of his rope of hope. He declared that he wished his eyes would be a fountain of tears so he could weep day and night because of the condition of his people. He even wished he could just run away because they were all treacherous adulterers who spoke lies and were not valiant for the truth. Then the Lord spoke that they only proceeded from evil to evil and didn't really know Him.[28] Truly no one can trust what the other says. God warned everyone to be aware of their neighbors, not even trusting a brother, for they were all deceivers and every neighbor was a slanderer. No one was speaking the truth, and they wearied themselves committing iniquity.[29] He went on in great detail how their tongues were like sharpened arrows, speaking deceit, and how they would speak peaceably with their neighbors but in their hearts they laid in wait for them. And the whole nation was like this![30]

The root of the problem was His own children had forsaken the Torah, His Law, and had not listened to His voice or walked in His ways but walked after the stubbornness of their own hearts. God said therefore that He would feed His children wormwood, give them water of gall to drink, and then scatter them among the nations, sending the sword after them until they were consumed.[31]

We close this chapter with some very sound advice from the Lord, telling us that if anyone wants to glory, let him glory in the fact that he understands and knows God. He is the One who exercises mercy and justice and righteousness, and that is what He delights in! The wise man should forget about glorying in his own wisdom or the mighty man in his own strength.[32]

Then we hear of the far-reaching judgment, with God stating that everyone was going to get punished, from the uncircumcised to the circumcised, even to the farthest corners of the earth, because those who were circumcised were uncircumcised in heart.[33] May all those who have ears to hear listen to what the Spirit is saying!

Let's summarize some thoughts.

Amazingly the prophets, priests, and pastors were the ones bringing judgment upon the people by their wicked ways. They manipulated God's Word to control the people. I believe God hates religion, and He is looking for a relationship. While many call themselves believers, we see the truth will be revealed when God judges professing believers along with all the unbelievers.

QUESTIONS

- What is the Lord telling you about Himself?
- What else has the Lord taught you?

CHAPTER 5

IT'S TIME TO WINNOW

JEREMIAH 15–16

AT THIS POINT, we've covered the many times God has told Jeremiah not even to think about praying for these rebellious people. Well, if you wanted anyone to even try and intercede for you, who would it be? Who is the most righteous person you could think of in the Bible whom you would want to pray for you in this time frame before Messiah? Does Moses or Samuel come to mind? Here is what God told Jeremiah. He told him that even if Moses and Samuel were standing before Him, His mind still wouldn't be favorable toward these people. Just cast the people out of His sight![1]

God decided He was going to appoint over them four forms of destruction: the sword to slay, the dogs to drag, and the birds of the heavens with the beasts of the earth to devour and destroy them. He was going to hand them over to trouble because of what Manasseh did in Jerusalem![2]

Now, wait a minute! Did God not forgive Manasseh? There's one thing we need to learn from history other than the fact that we never learn from history. The consequences of our sins have ripple effects that can go on for generations! Sure, forgiveness may come, but it's similar to when a mother abuses herself during pregnancy and the baby in the womb can still be negatively affected for life, whether the mom repents or not. Manasseh had caused many to err and turn from God's ways, and they in turn caused many others to grievously sin. And the cycle went on and on. Too often, when we sin, we think it is only about ourselves and we aren't hurting anybody but ourselves by what we do. Not so, my friend!

We have to remember that when Israel broke their covenantal relationship with God, it unleashed the consequences that came with it. So let's go to Leviticus 26 and see just what that entailed as it became so applicable to their time almost one thousand years later.

The good news was that if they obeyed Him, didn't make any idols or carved images, and kept His Sabbaths, then they would be blessed and would get the rain they so desperately needed in their desert climate. The land would yield its produce, and the trees would yield their fruit. There would be peace in the land, and no one would ever be afraid, with no evil beasts or enemies. Five of them would chase a hundred, and a hundred would put ten thousand to flight![3]

But the bad news was if they did not obey Him, despised His statutes, and broke His commandments, it wouldn't be pretty! The first thing was to appoint terror over them, accompanied by a wasting disease and fever. Then they would be defeated by their enemies, people who hated them would reign over them, and they would flee when no one was even chasing them.[4]

If they didn't repent, then they would be punished seven more times! He would break the pride of their power and make their heavens like iron and their land like brass. And if they still didn't obey, then another seven plagues would come according to their sins, and then He would send the wild beasts their way to rob them of their children and destroy their livestock, and their highways would be desolate.[5]

If none of this worked to reform them and they still walked contrary to God, they would be punished again, seven more times! This time it would be with the sword and pestilence and being delivered into the hands of the enemy.[6]

Finally God said if none of this worked and they still would not obey, they would be chastised seven more times! They would eat the flesh of their sons and daughters and cast their carcasses on the lifeless forms of their idols.[7] I can't think of anything more horrific than eating your own children.

We then find that even Israel's enemies would be astonished at the extent of the desolation. God declared in Leviticus that they needed to keep His Sabbaths, which refers to so much more than the seventh day of the week; it refers to all the appointed times that occur during the year as well as the seventh-year Sabbath for the land and the Jubilee year.

It was prophesied that if they did not obey, God would bring the land into desolation and Israel's enemies would be astonished at it all. God would then scatter them among the nations so the land would enjoy its Sabbaths.[8] This prophecy, from close to nine hundred years earlier, stated if Israel didn't keep the seventh-year Sabbath, allowing the land to rest, they would be in big trouble. For the previous 490 years they never let the land enjoy its Sabbath rest, so now they would be held captive in Babylon for seventy years, allowing the land to get caught up on its missing rest.

In the Book of Deuteronomy—the events of which occurred during the last month of Moses' life, when he renewed the covenant with the people—the Lord mentioned that every seventh year the debts were to be erased and any Hebrew servants were to be set free.[9] In the year before Nebuchadnezzar destroyed the temple, as we will soon be reading about in our decoding of Jeremiah, the people's disobedience to this command was the final straw for God.[10]

As I mentioned, God appointed four forms of destruction, and then He said that He would winnow them with a winnowing fork, and He was so upset that He had to destroy His own people since they refused to return from their ways.[11] I can't help but be reminded of when Yochanan the Immerser (John the Baptist) stated that someone was coming after him who was mightier than he was, referring to Yeshua. He said that Yeshua had a winnowing fork in His hand and would thoroughly clean out His threshing floor, gather His wheat into the barn, and burn up the chaff with unquenchable fire.[12]

Just a little later in the story, Yeshua told a parable about a man who sowed good seed in his field, but an enemy came and sowed bad seed in the same field. This is the parable of the wheat and the tares. The different seed here is referring to two types of people: the wicked and the righteous. The owner, being concerned for the wheat, said to wait for the harvest and then take out the tares first and burn them. Then, secondly, they were to gather the wheat and put it in the owner's barn.[13]

By waiting for harvest time, it would be much easier to separate the wheat from the tares. The wheat would be full of fruit and bows, while the tares would have no fruit and would stay perpendicular, standing out. But where is God's threshing floor and barn? Where exactly is the wheat taken? I find it interesting that the Temple Mount in Jerusalem was initially a threshing floor![14] I also find it interesting that the tares were to be reaped before the wheat was taken.

This coincides with another parable by Yeshua, in which two will be in a field, and one will be taken and the other left. Two will be grinding at a mill, and one will be taken and one left. The disciples asked where they would be taken, and Yeshua's response was where their carcass is, there the eagles will be gathered.[15]

In this specific case, I would prefer to be left behind! My take on this, and I am not dogmatic at all, is that we do know there will be unbelievers who survive the tribulation, entering the thousand-year reign, who will have to come up every year to keep the Feast of Tabernacles in Jerusalem or else they receive the plague and no rain.[16] Therefore, this verse refers specifically to the very wicked.

In the comparison parable of the wheat and the tares, we find the tares are taken first and then the wheat. So I see the very wicked being "raptured" to the battle of Armageddon.[17] Believers, represented by the wheat, will also be gathered together to the battle of Armageddon. The Temple Mount was a threshing floor first, if you remember. In Matthew 13:30, God gathers His wheat into His barn. So I see believers gathered together with Yeshua coming back to Jerusalem while there is also a harvest of the very wicked who are also transported there for the fight.

Let's return to Jeremiah. When the people came to him, asking him why the Lord pronounced this great disaster against them and what iniquity they could have possibly committed against the Lord to merit such evil, Jeremiah was instructed to tell them it was because their fathers forsook God and didn't keep His Law, and now they had done even worse as each one of them followed the dictates of their own evil hearts. No one listened or obeyed God anymore, so as He warned them—out they would go![18]

But next came a promise of God's mercy! The Lord declared that days were coming that would eclipse the exodus from Egypt, and it would be said that the Lord who brought up the children of Israel from all the places they had been driven still lives. God then promised He would send fishermen who would fish them back, and then many hunters would come and hunt them from every mountain and hill and out of the holes of the rocks.[19] This is the verse Messiah was referring to when He told the disciples they were to be fishers of men.[20]

Jeremiah saw the Gentiles coming to the Lord from the ends of the earth. I live in the Seattle, Washington, area. We definitely feel like we are at the end of earth in relation to where Israel is located! Washington is one of the most unchurched states in all of the United States. God always moves in the darkest corners and that is where we live. When that happens, the believing Gentiles are finally going to realize that they inherited lies from their fathers, things that were worthless and unprofitable, and they will realize that the Lord is God.[21]

THE PROPHET HABAKKUK

To get an even clearer idea of what times were like during Jeremiah's life, it is beneficial to check out what other prophets were saying to that generation. Let's look at the burden of Habakkuk. He had a big, driving question for God that he wanted answered. He implored God to tell him why He was not listening to him! He cried out about the violence going on. He saw plundering, strife, and contention, and he concluded that the Law was powerless and justice never goes forth. The wicked were surrounding the righteous so that perverse judgment proceeded.[22] Does this sound like our day or what?

The Gospel of Luke describes the generation that will see the return of the Messiah as being just like the days of Noah and Lot.[23] Do you know what the number-one reason was for God destroying the earth during Noah's day? God told Noah twice that it was because the earth was filled with violence.[24] This sounds exactly like the generation we are living in today.

God told Habakkuk to watch what was going on and be astounded because God was going to do something he wouldn't believe. He was going to raise up the Chaldeans to overtake other countries, and the Chaldeans were definitely a rotten bunch of people.[25] God told Habakkuk to grab a tablet and to write the vision he was getting from God and to make it very plain for whoever read it. The vision Habakkuk received is yet for an appointed time, yet it will surely come. Just wait for it because the just shall live by his faith.[26] Wow, do you see that? The whole idea of the just living by faith has always been an Old Testament concept! I can hardly wait for this next promise from the Lord through Habakkuk that one day—and I believe one day soon—the entire earth will be filled with the knowledge of the glory of the Lord as the waters cover the sea.[27] Definitely sounds like in the days of Noah!

We know there had been a major famine and drought going on during this time frame, and I find it compelling that no matter what, Habakkuk put his faith in the Lord. We find this when he stated that even when the fig tree wasn't blossoming, there wasn't any fruit on the vines, the fields weren't yielding any food, and there were no herds in the stalls, he was still going to rejoice in the God of his salvation. He declared that God was his strength.[28]

Let's summarize some thoughts.

Can you imagine being in a moral condition in which God tells people to not even pray for you? That is terrifying! Many believe that proclaiming Jesus gives them a coupon to sin all they want, and all they need to do is pull out their Jesus cards when needed while their hearts are never changed.

While God may punish His children, His purpose is always to get them to come to their senses and repent. He does this out of His love for them. When Israel returns in a way likened to the first Exodus, there will be an awakening among non-Jews to realize they have been taught lies by their fathers. They will no longer see through a glass darkly but will have a greater understanding of God. While believers suffer many trials and tribulations and the wicked seem to prosper, we need to keep our eyes on Yeshua, the author and finisher of our faith.

Questions

- What is the Lord telling you about Himself?

- What else has the Lord taught you?

CHAPTER 6

THE POTTER'S HOUSE

JEREMIAH 7, 18-19, AND 2

THE PEOPLE IN Jerusalem were trusting in the blessings of the covenant while ignoring the curses of the covenant. Why, the very temple of the Creator of the universe was in their midst! This wasn't their first time to misunderstand. Over a thousand years earlier, during the time of the judges, they took the ark of the covenant into battle against the Philistines. They imagined it to be some lucky charm, but they were roundly defeated and the ark was captured. Well, in Jeremiah's day they felt they were immune to defeat because they had the temple to trust in.

It was much like some of today's Christians, who believe having their little Jesus statue or even saying "magic words" such as "Jesus loves me" somehow makes them immune from God's judgments when they behave in the most ungodly ways. It's like they tell themselves, "Trouble is coming, so let me pull God out of my pocket and rebuke the enemy, and then I'll just put God away, as I can't have Him interrupting the good times!" This is what was happening in Jerusalem.

As we've already discussed, God was loudly speaking to the people, telling them to amend their ways. He even told them not to trust in the temple, yet all they could repeat was, "The temple of the LORD," over and over. God said those were lying words. It was only if they thoroughly amended their ways—properly executing judgment; not oppressing the stranger, fatherless, or widow; not shedding innocent blood; and not walking after other gods—that He would allow them to stay in the land.[1]

Next we find God asking the people whether they really believed they could steal, murder, commit adultery, swear falsely, and burn incense to Baal and other gods, and then stand before Him in the very house called by His name and say that they were delivered to do all these abominations. And the house called by His name had become a den of thieves![2] This was the very reference Yeshua used in His day about the rebuilt temple when He drove out all the moneychangers, exclaiming that His house was to be a house of prayer, but they had made it into a den of thieves![3] I hear this comment all the time within Christianity today that people believe they have been delivered to do every type of abomination because they are covered by the blood and the Law is done away with! They have a big surprise coming!

God told the people to go take a look at what He did to Shiloh because of the wickedness of the people. Again He told the people that He rose up early to speak to them, but they would not hear; He called them, and they didn't answer. He said that therefore He would destroy the house called by His name, in which they trusted.[4] Very soon God will judge the modern generation of believers who think the same way. It will be a case of "Can you hear Me now?"

God now wanted to bring out a very important point. He reminded them that when He delivered the people from Egypt, He didn't mention anything about burnt offerings or sacrifices. The only thing He commanded them was to obey His voice, and He would be their God, and they would be His people. The problem though is they did not listen then, and they weren't listening now; they had been going backward and not forward.[5]

God then declared again that He even got up early, sending all of His prophets to them, yet they refused to listen, followed the dictates of their own evil hearts, and went backward and not forward. All they did was stiffen their necks, doing worse than their fathers. God told Jeremiah to go ahead speak these words to them, even though they wouldn't obey Him. He told Jeremiah to give them a call, and he would see that they wouldn't answer him either.[6] It's like God was asking Jeremiah to walk in His shoes and see how it felt.

I don't think I can begin to fathom the extent of God's heartbreak as I cover what God revealed to Jeremiah about Himself next. He described the evil that the children of Judah had done, not only by setting their detestable things within the very house called by His name but also building the high places of Tophet in the Hinnom Valley, known as the Valley of Blood, to burn their own sons and daughters in the fire. God poured out His heart to Jeremiah, declaring He never commanded them to do that, and it never even entered His mind![7]

In the Hinnom Valley the fires were continually burning, and it became the garbage dump. It was also known as Gehenna, or hellfire.

We find Yeshua mentioning who the greatest were in the kingdom of heaven. He called a child to Himself and stated that unless His followers became like little children, they couldn't enter the kingdom of heaven. He told them they better not offend one of the little ones. Then He said that if your hand or foot offends you, cut it off, for that would be better than to be cast into everlasting fire with both hands and feet. And if your eye offends you, cut it out, for that would be better than to be cast into the hellfire with both eyes. And then again He stated they better not despise one of the little ones because their angels always behold the face of His Father in heaven.[8]

It was no accident that Yeshua mentioned Gehenna, or hellfire, in the context of condemning those who attacked children, treating them like garbage. They better be fearful because the children's angels are in face-to-face meeting with God! This pertains not only to the abortion issue but the sexual abuse of children that is rampant everywhere today—even in the church.

The word of the Lord came again to Jeremiah, saying that He was the potter and Israel was the clay in His hand, and He could do whatever He pleased with the clay. As a matter of fact all nations are but clay in His hands, and at the very instant He speaks against a nation to pluck it up, pull it down, or destroy it, if they repent, He will repent of the disaster He is sending.[9]

God informed Jeremiah that His own people had forgotten Him and stumbled by following their own ways. They left the ancient paths.[10] He was referring to His Torah. The people responded by coming together to devise plans against Jeremiah to smite him with their tongues and not heed any of his words.[11] Jeremiah responded by crying out to God again to go destroy them all![12]

This brings us to chapter 19 of Jeremiah, in which the Lord told Jeremiah it was time to go see the potter and take some of the elders of the people and some of the elders of the priests with him. He was to take them on a field trip to the Hinnom Valley, or Valley of Blood, which is by the entry of the Potsherd Gate.

At that significant place, he was now to proclaim the word of the Lord to the kings of Judah and the inhabitants of Jerusalem: God was bringing such a catastrophe on this place that the ears of whoever heard it would tingle. He was to tell them that because they had forsaken God, made Jerusalem an alien place, and filled the place with the blood of the innocents by burning their sons with fire for burnt offerings to Baal—which was never commanded or even came into His mind—the days were coming when that place would no longer be called Tophet or the Valley of the Son of Hinnom but the Valley of Slaughter.[13]

Did you recognize that phrase? Jeremiah said their "ears shall tingle" to remind them of two other times this phrase was used. It hearkened back to the destruction of the tabernacle at Shiloh, when God told the young boy Samuel when he heard from the Lord for the very first time that the two sons of the high priest, Eli, were extremely wicked and Eli allowed it.[14] The other time was at the beginning of Manasseh's reign, due to all of his abominations.[15]

Then Jeremiah was to break the flask in everyone's sight and tell them that God would break them and the city, as one breaks a potter's vessel, to the point it could not be made whole again. And there would be so many people buried in Tophet, there wouldn't be enough room for all of them! As matter of fact the whole city would be like Tophet because on every rooftop they had burned incense and poured out drink offerings to foreign gods.[16]

So Jeremiah left Tophet, stood in the court of the Lord's house, and declared to everyone there that the Lord of Hosts was bringing doom to Jerusalem because they all had stiff necks.[17] I don't know about you, but my next step would be to run for my life!

The Lord then inquired of the entire nation of Israel what injustice their fathers had found He had done that resulted in them going so far from Him. God mentioned that they didn't even ask where the Lord was, the God who brought them out of Egypt through the wilderness, a barren place of death where no one lives.[18] In other words, God was asking them if they could find any fault with Him when all He had done was show them good by delivering them from Egypt and carrying them on His shoulders as a father carries his son.[19]

The Lord then mentioned that even the priests didn't ask where the Lord was. They were the ones who were supposed to handle His Law, and they didn't even know God! The rulers were transgressing against Him, and the prophets were prophesying by Baal and walking after things that don't profit.[20] This is incredible!

The role of the priest was much more than serving in the temple. As a matter of fact there were so many priests that they were on a rotation so all of them could get a chance to serve in the temple. A priest would only serve two weeks a year in his regular rotation and then serve the three weeks of the year when the three main feasts were held: Passover, Shavuot/Pentecost, and Sukkot/Tabernacles. That's a total of five weeks a year.

It begs the question, What in the world did they do the other forty-seven weeks a year? They were supposed to get out from the four walls of the temple and teach the people the Torah! The priests were to be the teachers.[21] And only a small portion of the Levites were priests. What about all the other Levites who weren't priests? What in the world were they doing? The Levites' primary job was teaching the Law of God! They were scattered throughout all the tribes, just so everyone would have access to the knowledge of the Torah.[22]

It reminds me of a verse in Revelation that many people and pastors today misinterpret. It's the verse that talks about Yeshua standing at the door and knocking and saying that if anyone hears Him and opens the door, He will sup with him.[23] They use this verse to say the Lord knocks on the door of an unbeliever to open the door of his heart and believe. Sorry! It is a church door, the door of the Laodicean church, and everyone is ignoring Him, telling Him to go away as they are having church and they either don't even realize He has left or don't care!

God always is more upset at how His own kids treat Him than how the wicked do. Nobody really cares as much if the neighbors hate them compared to if their own family does! Yet we find the Lord declaring that His own people had committed two evils: one, by forsaking Him as the fountain of living waters, and two, by hewing out broken cisterns that hold no water.[24] The cisterns represent Egypt and Assyria, two countries they had relied on for help in time of war.[25]

The Lord told the people that even if they were to wash themselves with the strongest alkali, or the strongest acid, it wouldn't erase their sin because it was marked, or engraved, before Him. And yet they did not believe they had done anything wrong.[26] He stated that just as a thief was ashamed when caught in the act, Israel acted the same way. Therefore, in the time of their trouble, when they cried out and asked God to save them, God would tell them to go call on the gods they had made for themselves and worshipped and to let their idols save them.[27]

And yet again the heart of God was touched, and He asked the people if a maid could forget her ornaments or a bride her attire. If not, then why had His own people forgotten Him days without number![28]

How many of you are hurt when you are forgotten by people you love? Have you ever felt forgotten by someone you thought loved you? No communication at all for days, weeks, months, or how about years? Have you ever done many wonderful things for someone and never heard back? If so, you can begin to feel God's heartbreak over His kids.

Frustratingly the people claimed to be innocent and expected God to turn away His anger. So God declared His case against them because they believed they had not sinned![29] This reminds me of the verse in which Yeshua told some of the Pharisees that if they were blind, they would have no sin, but because they claimed to see, their sin remained.[30]

During this same time frame, as Josiah was still king, we find the kingdom of Assyria, with its capital in Nineveh, was finally about to fall to the Babylonians. All of these events Jeremiah was personally witnessing, knowing the people of Israel were next!

NINEVEH

The prophet Nahum came on the scene, declaring his burden against Nineveh. He was declaring that God is a jealous God who takes vengeance on His enemies. Yet God is slow to anger and great in power, not at all acquitting the wicked.[31] Nahum went on to say that God was judging Nineveh because it was a bloody city, full of lies and robbery.[32] Sounds a lot like the same reasons God judged Jerusalem and may very well judge a city next to each of us!

We are about to end our study of King Josiah and move on to the unfolding saga of Jeremiah's experiences. So let's look at the end of King Josiah's life. First a little bit of history. When the Assyrian capital of Nineveh was overrun by the Babylonians around 612 BC, they quickly moved their capital to Harran, which is in modern-day Turkey. When the Babylonians captured that city two years later on their advance, the Assyrians then moved their forces to Carchemish.

In 609 BC the Egyptian army of Pharaoh Necho II was being delayed at Megiddo by the forces of King Josiah! There were two major historical battles at Carchemish, one in 609 BC and the other in 605 BC. The one around May or June of 605 BC is most commonly referred to as the battle of Carchemish, and military history buffs may enjoy reading about it as it was one of the most decisive battles in world history. After the war Egypt was reduced to a second-rate power, and the Babylonian Empire, after conquering Israel, attempted to take over Egypt as well.

We find the biblical record of the first battle in Chronicles. Josiah went out to stop Pharaoh from helping the Assyrians against Babylon. Pharaoh sent messengers to King Josiah, asking him what he was doing, because he had no fight with Israel; he just needed to pass through. Pharaoh added the comment to Josiah that he was only following the Word of the Lord, as He was the one who told him to help and to hurry up! He told King Josiah he needed to cease opposing God, who was with him, so that God wouldn't destroy King Josiah.[33]

Josiah disguised himself so he could continue to fight instead of listening to the words of Pharaoh from the mouth of God! He was now fighting Pharaoh in the Valley of Megiddo. The archers shot King Josiah, and he was grievously wounded and told his servants to get him out of there! They took him out of his chariot, threw him in another, and went off to Jerusalem, where Josiah died. All of Judah, Jerusalem, and even Jeremiah mourned the death of Josiah. Jeremiah even wrote a song of grief for Josiah and all the songwriters included Josiah's name in their songs of grief.[34]

KING JOSIAH DIES; KING JEHOAHAZ REIGNS THREE MONTHS

It was 609 BC, and Babylon had already been on the march. In 612 BC Nineveh fell to Babylon. In 610 BC Harran fell to Babylon. King Josiah died in a battle against Pharaoh, and now Pharaoh was jumping into Israeli politics. We then find that after King Josiah was killed, the people of the land took his son Jehoahaz, anointed him, and made him king in his father's place.[35]

Jehoahaz was twenty-three years old when he was made king and reigned an entire three months! As we discover why this happened, you will see a real soap opera taking place—a lot of palace intrigue, along with some cloak and dagger! Jeremiah watched all of this unfold. This can get very confusing, but try to follow along with me.

Jehoahaz's father was Josiah, and his mother was Hamutal, the daughter of another Jeremiah of Libnah. Jehoahaz was evil, and when Pharaoh Necho came to Jerusalem, he bound Jehoahaz and hauled him off to Egypt, where he died. Pharaoh then decided who would be king. He made Israel pay tribute in the amount of one hundred talents of silver and a talent of gold. Pharaoh made Josiah's other son, Eliakim, king, and changed his name to Jehoiakim, who more than willingly paid the taxes.[36] But wait! There's more! We now find Jehoiakim was twenty-five years old when he began to reign, and he reigned eleven years in Jerusalem.[37]

Why would Israel anoint Jehoahaz as king when he had an older brother who was twenty-five years old? Were they showing a preference in bypassing the firstborn? Well, it just so happens they were both firstborn—same father but different mothers! Jehoiakim's mother was Zebudah, the daughter of Pedaiah of Rumah![38]

Can you imagine Israel's insult to Zebudah, who definitely had the firstborn, when she was rejected as queen mother? She was thrilled that Pharaoh righted the wrong in her mind, and she made sure that her son would support Pharaoh and pay the taxes!

I also want to jump ahead for a second with a tidbit of information we will come back to for a point of reference. Jehoiakim was twenty-five years old and would be king for eleven years. He also had a son named Jehoiachin, who was seven years old. It just so happens that Jehoahaz—who was just deposed, was hauled off to Egypt, and died—had a little brother named Mattaniah (later renamed Zedekiah), who was ten years old at the time. Which mother would win the next round? We will see!

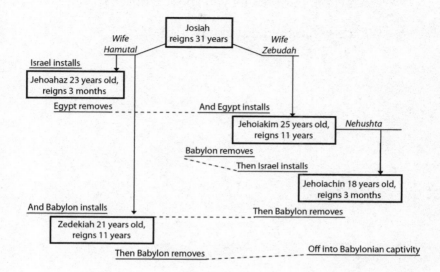

Let's summarize some thoughts.

Israel was relying on the physical temple to be a deterrent to disaster. The historical pattern is that God will destroy every temple that is to house His presence if it becomes defiled. His children were giving only lip service to God while their hearts were far from Him. Amazingly, even the very ones who were teaching the laws of the Torah didn't know that God wasn't even present. It is unbelievable to me how those in leadership treated children. This is so much like it is today. What stands out to me is just how deceived people can be in thinking they are in a relationship with God and it is the furthest thing from the truth. We also see how sometimes the children of this world (Pharaoh) hear from God better than God's own people. It is wise to keep a humble heart and try to even listen to our enemies.

QUESTIONS

- What is the Lord telling you about Himself?
- What else has the Lord taught you?

CHAPTER 7

KING JEHOIAKIM'S FIRST YEARS

JEREMIAH 26–27 AND 25

TIME HAD BEEN flying for Jeremiah. He was now around forty-one years old. It had been eighteen years since the Lord called him at the age of twenty-three. He had seen war, famine, drought, the ugly transition of power, hatred from every side, the greatest Passover ever held, and revival. King Jehoiakim, who witnessed the revival as a child and at bar mitzvah age likely watched his father rend his clothes from top to bottom at hearing the warnings from the word of the Lord, just might act in kind and disaster might be averted. Jehoiakim reigned for eleven years, and in this chapter we will focus on his first three years as king.

At the beginning of Jehoiakim's reign the Lord told Jeremiah to stand in the court of the house of the Lord and speak to everyone who came to worship all the words the Lord would command him, not leaving out a single word. This was in the hope that they would turn from their wicked ways, allowing God to repent of the disaster that He was bringing upon them.[1]

God always warns before He brings judgment. He is never willing that any should perish, and He loves showing mercy whenever we change our ways. But God will never override our free will.

So now there was the hope in a new administration, and maybe there would be another revival! It was 608 BC; the prophet Ezekiel and the prophet Daniel were both likely in their teens. They were listening to the words of Jeremiah.

Once again Jeremiah was told to warn the people that if they did not listen to God, walk in His Law that was set before them, and listen to the servants He was sending to them (such as Jeremiah), He would make His house like Shiloh and make the city of Jerusalem like a curse to all the nations of the earth.[2] God lovingly humbled Himself and pleaded with mankind to amend their ways because He did not want to bring harm. As a loving parent not wanting to discipline His children, God was giving them yet another chance.

So what happened? Everyone heeded the warnings, thanked Jeremiah, praised the Lord, and went home rejoicing in the fact that disaster had been averted? Not so! When all of his fellow priests and prophets and all the people heard Jeremiah speak these words in the house of the Lord, everyone pounced on him yelling, "You're a dead man!" One of the reasons was because he alluded to the destruction of the tabernacle in Shiloh that had stood for 369 years and was actually directly insulting them.[3] The reason the tabernacle was destroyed, according to Jewish tradition, was because of the wickedness of the high priest Eli's sons, Hophni and Phinehas. The people understood Jeremiah to be saying it was because of the wickedness of the priests of his day that the temple would be destroyed.

Jeremiah was totally surrounded in the house of the Lord by an angry mob.[4] The princes of Judah heard the commotion, so they left the king's house and sat down at the new gate to hear what was going on. The priests and prophets proclaimed that Jeremiah deserved to die for prophesying against Jerusalem.[5] Jeremiah responded with a don't-shoot-the-messenger plea, reminding them, "The LORD sent me to prophesy against this house and against this city all the words that ye have heard!"[6] He told them that all they had to do was repent and obey God, and the Lord would repent of the evil He was planning. Then Jeremiah, after setting forth his case humbly, said he was in their hands and for them to do whatever seemed right. But he also warned them that if they put him to death, they would bring his innocent blood on their heads, on the city, and on the people, because it really was God who sent him.[7]

Fortunately for Jeremiah the rulers and the people told the priests and prophets that they believed Jeremiah spoke the word of the Lord and was not worthy of death. Then some of the elders stood up and reminded everybody that Micah had prophesied that Zion would be plowed like a field and Jerusalem would become heaps, and nobody tried to kill him. Even King Hezekiah had listened and repented, causing the Lord to repent of the evil He was going to send back then. By killing Jeremiah, they would be doing great evil against their souls.[8]

Interestingly enough another prophet foretold the same thing as Jeremiah, and Jehoiakim sent his mighty men to kill this prophet. They chased him into Egypt and hauled him back to King Jehoiakim, who killed him and threw his body into the graves of the common people. But Jeremiah was being protected by the hand of Ahikam.[9]

Why is this significant? Ahikam was the son of Shaphan, and Shaphan was the scribe who, when they had found the Law of the Lord during the eighteenth year of King Josiah's reign, read it before the king.[10] It just so happened that Ahikam was also the father of Gedaliah, and Nebuchadnezzar would appoint Gedaliah to be governor in the near future before he would be murdered by a band of Jewish rebels![11]

As a sidenote for those who might not know, Gedaliah is huge in history as well as modern day. Every year for the last two thousand five hundred years, there has been a fast day remembering the death of Gedaliah who died on Rosh Hashanah. This shows the linkage of a righteous family in the midst of all the rebelliousness taking place.

Let's take a moment to catch up on a little of the world news of the time. The year 608 BC was Jehoiakim's first year as king, and he was beholden to Egypt who was still fighting with Assyria to hold back Nabopolassar, the king of Babylonia. Three years later, in 605 BC, Nebuchadnezzar, who was not yet king, besieged Jerusalem. At this time, the prophet Joel jumped into the prophetic roundtable, and we will soon be hearing from him in our decoding of Jeremiah.

Nebuchadnezzar began his reign after defeating Egypt in the battle of Carchemish and returning to Babylon in the spring after his father's death on August 15 of 605 BC. Based on this timeline, there is a possibility that while besieging Jerusalem, Nebuchadnezzar heard he would become king.

So here we are in 605 BC, which is the third year of Jehoiakim, and what do we find happening?

> In the third year of the reign of Jehoiakim king of Judah came Nebuchadnezzar king of Babylon unto Jerusalem, and

besieged it. And the Lord gave Jehoiakim king of Judah into his hand, with part of the vessels of the house of God: which he carried into the land of Shinar to the house of his god; and he brought the vessels into the treasure house of his god.

—DANIEL 1:1–2

Egypt had been minimized, Jerusalem had been invaded, and look at what else happened: some of the Hebrew children were hauled off to Babylon, including Daniel, along with Shadrach, Meshach, and Abednego, whose real names were Hananiah, Mishael, and Azariah. (In captivity they were given Babylonian names, as was Daniel, who became Belteshazzar.) This part of the story of Daniel took place during the third year of Jehoiakim. The fourth year of Jehoiakim, which we will explore in the next chapter, is considered the first year of Nebuchadnezzar, and does it ever get crazy from here!

You might have imagined the stories of Daniel and the three Hebrew children being thrown in the fiery furnace as happening after the temple was destroyed. Not at all. Much of the story of Daniel happened ten to seventeen years before the temple was destroyed by Nebuchadnezzar!

We now come upon a very crazy verse: Jeremiah 27:1. As I mentioned before, some translators intentionally mistranslated a name in their different versions of the Bible. This is why you have to rely on the Hebrew, not the English. Some translations say it was in the beginning of the reign Jehoiakim, and others say it was in the beginning of Zedekiah.

These two kings' beginnings were eleven years apart, so which is right? The Hebrew plainly says it was Jehoiakim. So why do the translators of some versions of the Bible say it was Zedekiah? It's because they think there had to be an error in the Hebrew Scripture. It begs the question, Why not translate it accurately and note their opinions instead of mistranslating it based on their assumptions?

It can be confusing because if you continue reading verses 2–3, it accurately mentions Zedekiah. I do not feel I have the authority to edit God's Word, so I leave it as is and try to understand what was happening. Others feel the same, as many Bible translations do keep it as Jehoiakim. I believe it was a prophecy of a future event that Jeremiah was to accomplish at the time specified. So here we go!

We see that in the beginning of Jehoiakim's reign the Lord told Jeremiah to make for himself bonds and yokes, put them on his neck, and send them off to other nations by the hand of messengers who came to Jerusalem to Zedekiah, king of Judah.[12] So Jeremiah got a preview of who would be the next king, and then he had to wait for the appropriate time.

The other crazy thing is that some of the chapters within Jeremiah give different time frames and cover different years. Jeremiah 27 is one of these strange chapters that we will revisit later. We are going to jump into chapter 25 now, in which we can clearly see what year it is.

In Jeremiah 25 we find out that the fourth year of Jehoiakim corresponded to the first year of Nebuchadnezzar. Jeremiah drew a very significant timeline for us. He told us that from the thirteenth year of Josiah to that very day, it had been twenty-three years since the word of the Lord had come to him.[13] Jeremiah was twenty-three when he started, and it had been twenty-three years, making him forty-six. For twenty-three years Jeremiah had been getting up early and speaking to them, and for twenty-three years they had not listened.

Remember, not only Jeremiah but the Lord had also continually risen early to speak to the people, and they had never listened to Him since they came out of Egypt. In this chapter, we see one verse after another in which God again said He had risen early, sending them His servants the prophets. I don't know about you, but when I get up early, it's because I either have an exciting adventure ahead or something of extreme importance. This just demonstrates the importance God puts on His kids returning home, back into a relationship with their Creator.

Then the Lord proclaimed that Nebuchadnezzar was His servant, and the Lord would bring him against Israel and all the nations around her. He declared that Israel and the surrounding nations would become an astonishment, a hissing and perpetual desolation as prophesied in the Torah. We also read a prophecy that the nations would serve Babylon seventy years. Then afterward, God would punish the king of Babylon and make it a perpetual desolation.[14] Payback was coming!

God then told Jeremiah that all the nations would drink of the wine cup of His fury.[15] This is the same imagery the Book of Revelation recorded, when an angel declared that Babylon was fallen because she made all the nations drink the wine of the wrath of her fornication. This was followed by an angel proclaiming with a loud voice that anyone who takes the mark of the beast will also drink of the wine of the wrath of God.[16] I find it an interesting parallel that seventy years have now been accomplished since Israel's nationhood. Will God now bring this judgment from the Book of Revelation about in our time?

God said that every nation on earth would drink of the cup of His wrath, because if He made Jerusalem, the very city called by His name, drink from the cup of His wrath for all their evil, then why should the other nations go unpunished for all of their evil? God was now calling for a sword upon all the inhabitants of the earth.[17]

In Seattle, where I currently live, I don't hear thunder very often the way I did when I lived in the Midwest. There, every spring brings rip-roaring thunderstorms with instantaneous cracks of lightning, often followed by supersonic booms of thunder that send everyone to the ceiling. Perhaps you know what I am talking about. You immediately collect your wits and settle down, thankful you survived.

Even more unsettling than thunder would be the sound of a lion's roar. If you were out in the brush of South Africa one night, and all of a sudden you heard a thunderingly loud roar of a lion just a few yards away, how would you feel? There would be no settling down but rather a melting into a fetal position!

Even that is nothing compared to when the Lion of the tribe of Judah will roar from on high and utter His voice from His holy habitation! He is going to give a shout against all the inhabitants of the earth that will be heard around the world.[18] He is going to raise up a great whirlwind from the coasts of the earth, and the slain will be scattered from one end of the earth to the other, and the dead won't be lamented, gathered, or even buried.[19]

JEHOIAKIM—11 YEARS

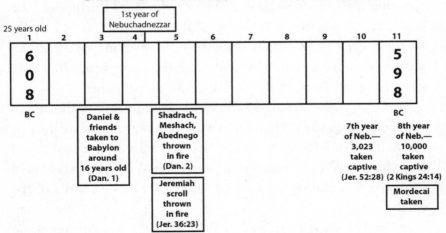

Let's summarize some thoughts.

God rose early in the morning and had His prophets rising early in the morning because He saw the importance of getting the message to His people, warning them of impending disaster. Daniel and friends were hauled off to Babylon in the third year of Jehoiakim. Jehoiakim's fourth year was Nebuchadnezzar's first year, and in the following year, the fifth year of Jehoiakim, the three Hebrew children were thrown into the fiery furnace. It was prophesied that the cup of wrath Israel experienced would be placed into the hands of the nations after seventy years. The seventy years of Israel's modern-day rebirth has now passed, and I wonder if history will repeat itself.

Questions

- What is the Lord telling you about Himself?

- What else has the Lord taught you?

CHAPTER 8

THE CRITICAL FOURTH AND FIFTH YEARS

JEREMIAH 22, 45, AND 36

I N THE LAST chapter, which covered Jeremiah 25, we learned that in the fourth year of Jehoiakim's reign, Nebuchadnezzar began his reign. But in the third of Jehoiakim, Nebuchadnezzar besieged Jerusalem and took captives, including Daniel and the other Hebrew children, as we find in Daniel 1:1. The next three chapters we will cover in the Book of Jeremiah (chapters 22, 45, and 36) all happened in Jehoiakim's fourth year. So you can see how out of sequence that book is. Chaos not only happens in his fourth year but also the fourth year of Zedekiah—and there was something about

Zedekiah's fourth year that I have found to be just as explosive. But first let's decode Jehoiakim's fourth year.

This time the Lord told Jeremiah to take a field trip to the house of the king of Judah and speak a word there. The Lord informed Jeremiah that if he and the nation exercised proper judgment, lived righteously, delivered the oppressed, and avoided wrongdoing, violence to the fatherless and widows, and shedding innocent blood, then kings would sit on the throne of David and all would be great. But if they didn't, God promised to turn them into a heap of ruin.[1] And when the nations asked why, they would be told because Israel forsook God and worshipped other gods. Then the Lord made it a little more personal by mentioning Josiah's other son, Jehoahaz, called Shallum here, and recounting the way he was hauled off to Egypt to die.[2]

Jehoiakim then heard what his father, Josiah, did to get to know God. His father pursued judgment and justice. He judged the cause of the poor and needy, and that is how he got to know God. But Jehoiakim's desire was only covetousness, shedding innocent blood, oppressing others, and being violent.[3] It was all about him.

Knowing God is more than an intellectual understanding; it is putting Torah into action. Jeremiah informed us that knowing God involves exercising lovingkindness, judgment, and righteousness in the earth, because that is what pleases God.[4]

If I were Jeremiah, standing in front of the king, I'm not sure I would have continued, because the Lord was about to really bring it home regarding what He thought of Jehoiakim. Would you? Jeremiah opened his mouth and uttered the words:

> Therefore, thus saith the LORD concerning Jehoiakim the son of Josiah king of Judah; They shall not lament for him, saying, Ah, my brother! or, Ah sister! they shall not lament for him, saying, Ah lord! or, Ah his glory! He shall be buried

with the burial of an ass, drawn and cast forth beyond the gates of Jerusalem.

—JEREMIAH 22:18–19

Then came a curse that his son Jeconiah, who was called Coniah for short, would be given into the hands of Nebuchadnezzar and cast out with his mother into another country.[5] Now you understand why I said that if I were Jeremiah, I would have turned and run for sure!

The Lord instructed them to record this man as if he were childless, because he would not prosper and none of his seed would rule on the throne of David.[6] While none of his seed ever ruled on the throne, he did have a son who played a part in Israel's future.

Three generations later the returnees from Babylon were headed by a man named Zerubbabel, the son of Shealtiel, the son of Jeconiah![7] On the twenty-first day of the seventh month, the Lord told the prophet Haggai to tell Zerubbabel, the son of Shealtiel, that the new house they were building would be filled with the glory of God.[8] It just so happened that the twenty-first day of the seventh month is the last day of Sukkot, the same day when Yeshua would later stand up and cry out that all who were thirsty should come to Him![9]

But getting back to Jeremiah, I'm telling you this is one of the most incredible years of biblical history. In Jeremiah chapter 36 we see that in this fourth year of Jehoiakim, the Lord told Jeremiah to write on a scroll all the words that He had spoken against Israel, against Judah, and against all the nations, from the days of Josiah up to that time.[10] That was twenty-three years of messages up to that point!

I guess the Lord wanted to make sure they had a record of what they heard so they would never forget. Because Jeremiah did what the Lord said, you are now blessed and able to read these very historic messages! It's a permanent picture of God's heart as He declared that the sole purpose of the warning was in hope that the house of Judah would hear it and repent so God could forgive their iniquity and sin.[11]

Jeremiah called Baruch, the son of Neriah, and Baruch had the fun task of writing from the mouth of Jeremiah all the words of the Lord from the last twenty-three years. Jeremiah was being detained and couldn't go into the house of the Lord, so Baruch entered the house of the Lord and read the word of the Lord from the mouth of Jeremiah that was written in the scroll. He was to read it on fast days when the people were coming from their cities to the temple so that if they were praying and presenting their supplications, maybe everyone would repent and God wouldn't have to bring the impending disaster.[12] I'm sure Baruch was thinking, "Woe is me," but he did it! He probably felt he would die at their hands!

So a time was coming to Israel just like what we witnessed in America after 9/11 when everyone ran to God after a disaster. Nebuchadnezzar had taken captives, and it was time to run to the temple with fasting and prayer.

THE PROPHET JOEL

I need to bring in the prophet Joel now. Nebuchadnezzar was characterized as a lion coming to destroy Jerusalem.[13] Well, Joel also described him this way when he spoke the word of the Lord.

> For a nation is come up upon my land, strong, and without number, whose teeth are the teeth of a lion, and he hath the cheek teeth of a great lion.
>
> —JOEL 1:6

Joel was telling the people to seek God! He even told them to sanctify a fast and to call a solemn assembly, gathering the elders and all the inhabitants to the house of God to cry out, for the day of the Lord was at hand and as a destruction of the Almighty it would come![14] Then he told them to blow a trumpet in Zion and sound the alarm, for the Lord was coming![15] God then told the people to turn to Him with all their hearts, with fasting, with weeping, and with mourning, rending their hearts and not their garments, for He is gracious and merciful, slow to anger, and of great kindness.[16]

This was a pivotal moment in history. Joel was working in tandem with Jeremiah and the Lord concerning this fasting day, which was also when Baruch was to read from the scroll. Joel told the priests that they needed to be weeping between the porch and the altar and crying out to God to spare His people.[17]

If you read Jeremiah 45, you discover that this was going on just before Baruch was coming in to speak. When Baruch had written these words from the mouth of Jeremiah, in the fourth year of Jehoiakim, listen to what the Lord said to Baruch through Jeremiah: "You said, 'Woe is me now!'"[18] Can you believe it? Then he told Baruch not even to think about seeking great things for himself. He told Baruch this place was history, but he would survive.[19]

When God orders people to fast, something has to be going on or coming down! So exactly when did this day of fasting take place? At this time, the only day of fasting on the biblical calendar was Yom Kippur. The other four fasting days that have been observed for the past 2,500 years all have had to do with the destruction of the temple, which hadn't happened yet at the time of Baruch. This is why I previously pointed out that some of Daniel's story and the story of the three Hebrew children being thrown into the fiery furnace in Babylon happened before the temple was destroyed. They were thrown in the furnace in the fifth year of Jehoiakim, which was almost eighteen years before Nebuchadnezzar destroyed the temple.

So in the fifth year of Jehoiakim, in the ninth month, a fast was proclaimed before the Lord.[20] The ninth month, known as the month of Kislev, occurs in the winter, usually equivalent to our December. It is the month of Hanukkah! That same day, Baruch was in the house of the Lord, reading the words of the Lord from the mouth of Jeremiah. One of the listeners told all the princes what he had heard, and they requested that Baruch come and read it to them. After hearing the word, they were terrified and decided to tell the king. They asked Baruch how he got this information, and he told them it came directly from Jeremiah's mouth and he wrote it down. The princes told him he had better quickly hide and not tell anyone where.[21] When the princes told the king what they had heard, he sent a man by the name of Jehudi to fetch the scroll and read it to him.[22]

Get ready because all the pieces are about to come together.

As we've learned, Jehoiakim was a bar mitzvah boy he heard the word of the Lord read to his father, King Josiah, who then tore his garments in fear and repentance. Would Jehoiakim respond in kind?

King Jehoiakim was in his winter house, and there was a fire on the hearth burning before him. When Jehudi had read three or four columns, he cut it with a knife and cast it into the fire until all the roll was consumed. He was not afraid, nor did he tear his garments, and neither did any of his servants that heard the words.[23]

You have to remember it was the fifth year of Jehoiakim, which was the second year of Nebuchadnezzar, that the word of the Lord was thrown into the fire. It just so happens that the second year of Nebuchadnezzar's reign was when Nebuchadnezzar had his troublesome dream, and Daniel interpreted it for him.[24]

Nebuchadnezzar built his image of gold, and because the three Hebrew boys refused to worship it, they were thrown into the fiery furnace. King Nebuchadnezzar was astonished when he saw not only the three men who were cast into the fire walking around but also a fourth man walking around with them.[25] This is just too much! The word of the Lord was thrown into the fire in Jerusalem, and now the word of the Lord (Yeshua Messiah) appeared in the fire of Babylon! In Jerusalem three or four columns of the word of the Lord were thrown into the fire, and in Babylon three or four people appeared in the fiery furnace. Good thing people were fasting and praying!

Interestingly enough, different translations describe what was thrown into the fire in Jerusalem as either leaves or columns of the scroll. The Hebrew word is *delet*, which actually means door. There is an interesting parallel between people and doors. In two different verses people are compared to doors.[26] We also know Yeshua is likened to a door,[27] and the word of the Lord is compared to a fire.[28] So I find all of the symbolism fascinating.

The king demanded that Jeremiah and Baruch be seized, but they were hidden away, and the Lord instructed Jeremiah to have another copy made. God made an addendum to the words of the last scroll, informing Jehoiakim that none of his descendants would sit on the throne of David, that his dead body would be cast out into the open, and not only would he be punished but so would his family, his servants, and the inhabitants of Jerusalem. They would experience all of the doom God had pronounced against them because they did not heed the warnings.[29]

Let's summarize some thoughts.

God's servants have to be bold when proclaiming the word of the Lord, but they better be sure it is His word and not their own feelings or thoughts. We must be careful not to add or subtract from God's word.

I find it amazing that the same year that as three or four columns of the word of the Lord are thrown into the fire in Jerusalem we find that three, no, four people were found in the fiery furnace of Babylon—especially since we see in the opening verses of the Gospel of John that Yeshua is compared to being the "Word." Here we have the Word of the Lord appearing in the fiery furnace in Babylon the same year the word of the Lord was thrown in the fire in Jerusalem. This is why having a timeline and connecting the different books during the same timeline is so important.

QUESTIONS

- What is the Lord telling you about Himself?

- What else has the Lord taught you?

CHAPTER 9

THE RECHABITES

JEREMIAH 13 AND 35

H ERE WE ARE in the middle of the eleven-year reign of Jehoiakim, and we find that the Lord instructed Jeremiah to put on a linen belt, wear it to the river Euphrates, and hide it under a rock. Jeremiah did what the Lord said, and after many days he was told to go back and fetch it. When he did, he saw that it was all marred and good for nothing.[1]

The Lord then informed Jeremiah that it would be after this manner that He would mar the pride of Judah and the great pride of Jerusalem. God really expressed His feelings to Jeremiah as He referred to the evil people who refused to hear His words. God had wanted Israel and Judah to be as the belt while it was being worn, cleaving to Him for their glory, but they refused and wouldn't listen. But because they had walked in the imagination of their hearts, worshipping other gods and serving them, they were going to be just like the belt after it had been hidden under the rock, all marred and good for nothing.[2]

When God releases His wrath on earth, I don't want to be anywhere around. It reminds me of times when I was a child and my dad got mad about something. It didn't matter what he was mad about; all nine of us kids bolted in every direction like a bunch of startled cats. God's anger is always justified, always done at the correct time, and always done in the right measure, but even so, I would be out of there.

I can't help but feel the tension as I read that God told Jeremiah to fill every bottle with wine and explain to the people that He would fill them with drunkenness—from the kings to the priests to the prophets to all the inhabitants—and then smash them into each other without pity or mercy until they were destroyed.[3]

God's heartbreak over his children comes through loud and clear in the next few verses, and we find the Lord calling out for them to hear and give ear. In the Book of Revelation we read over and over the exhortation, "He who has an ear, let him hear."[4] In Hebrew the word for *hear* actually means both to hear and obey, or as I would say, to pay very close attention.

God told them to not be proud but to give glory to the Lord before He caused darkness to come and envelop them, making them stumble around, and while they would be looking for light, He would turn it into the shadow of death and make it even gross darkness.[5] And if they still wouldn't hear, He said, "My soul shall weep in secret places for your pride; and mine eye shall weep sore, and run down with tears, because the LORD's flock is carried away captive."[6]

In the next verse, God wanted Jeremiah to tell the king and queen to humble themselves and sit down because their principalities were about to be taken down—even the crown of their glory![7]

God Is in Control

I have to stop and add something here because as I write this, the world is reeling in the midst of what is called the coronavirus. As I've mentioned, I live in the Tacoma-Seattle area, which was at one time the epicenter for the virus in the United States. At this moment the entire state has been told that all restaurants are to be closed; there are to be no meetings over ten people, basically shutting down all churches; and everyone age sixty and older should self-quarantine. The store shelves are being emptied faster than you can imagine, with people fighting over toilet paper. It's a whole new world.

I don't just believe the Bible; I *really* believe the Bible! I know there is a Creator, and the Scriptures plainly declare in Ecclesiastes 3:1 that "to every thing there is a season, and a time to every purpose under the heaven." So this begs the question "What is the purpose of the coronavirus going on a rampage around the world at this very time?" God has a purpose for everything that happens. Only mankind can try to uncover the meaning. Is there a divine message that we need to discern?

Many are endeavoring to figure out how to cope with this virus when at this time there are no test kits, there is no antidote, and there seems to be no way to stop its spread other than to isolate yourself, hide in a bunker, or at best stay six feet away from everyone as you soak yourself in hand sanitizer. Few people stop to think if there may be a divine message in all of this. Here are some of my thoughts as to the possible clues.

We have been experiencing the greatest bull market in history over the last four years. Mankind has been consumed with the hustle and bustle of making money that they have taken all the credit for. They have forgotten to take a time-out to thank God. The Scriptures tell us in Deuteronomy 8:18 that it is God who gives you the power to get wealth. We need to remember, as the Bible says in Job 1:21, we came into this world naked, we are leaving naked, and it is the Lord who gives to us, and it is the Lord who takes away. We are not in control.

With this coronavirus, the big thing is to make sure you keep your hands clean. Let's put a spiritual application to this and remember Psalm 24:4, which states that the one who ascends to the house of the Lord is the one who has clean hands and a pure heart. I've heard it said that as a parent puts a child into time-out when he has been bad to give him time to reflect on the consequences of his misbehavior, maybe God is forcing humanity into a time-out for us to rethink our own priorities. I also believe this could be a dry run for bigger things that may be coming our way over the next ten years, giving us time to repent and return to God.

So back to our verse where God says the principalities would be taken down, even the crown of their glory. We know that it is from the Latin word *corōna* that we get the English word *crown*. This virus forces us to ponder what happens when man tries to wear the crown that belongs to God Himself. We get plagued! There are different Hebrew words for *crown*, one of them being Keter, כתר, as found in Esther 1:11, where Queen Vashti is asked to appear before the king and his party wearing nothing but the royal crown.

It just so happens this Hebrew word has a numerical value of 620; every Hebrew letter has a numerical value much like Roman numerals. There is what is commonly called the crown of the Torah, and every Torah scroll has a crown. It is to tell mankind that there is a King of kings and Lord of lords who reigns supreme. Every Jew knows there are actually 613 commandments, or *mitzvoth*, that God gave the Jewish people, and there are also what are known as the seven laws that were given to Noah for all of mankind to follow. Interestingly this also adds up to 620!

Sadly, in the Book of Revelation, instead of repenting when God is trying to get man's attention, all the people do is harden their hearts as Pharaoh did when the plagues were coming fast and furiously at him!

I want to bring something else out at this time that I believe really needs to be understood, and then we will get back to our story with the bottles of wine. Many of us are familiar with the Bible verses about pride going before destruction and how it is better to be of a humble spirit with the lowly.[8] If I were to ask what the sin of Sodom was that God saw fit to destroy it, many would think it was sodomy or homosexuality.

If you remember, Abraham's heart was not to judge the city, but he was trying to save it, hoping God would spare it if he could find at least ten righteous living within it. Sure, Sodom had a lot of sins, but there is a difference between the root and the flower. What was the underlying root cause? Ezekiel, who was living during the time of Jeremiah, informed us:

> Behold, this was the iniquity of thy sister Sodom, pride, fulness of bread, and abundance of idleness was in her and in her daughters, neither did she strengthen the hand of the poor and needy. And they were haughty, and committed abomination before me: therefore I took them away as I saw good.
>
> —EZEKIEL 16:49–50

Notice the priority. Number one was pride, followed by fullness of bread and an abundance of idleness, which in common lingo would be "fat and lazy." Sodom didn't help those in need but was haughty and committed abominations. Speaking of abominations, if we go to the Book of Proverbs, we find God's top seven abominations.

> These six things doth the LORD hate: yea, seven are an abomination unto him: a proud look, a lying tongue, and hands that shed innocent blood, an heart that deviseth wicked imaginations, feet that be swift in running to mischief, a false witness that speaketh lies, and he that soweth discord among brethren.
>
> —PROVERBS 6:16–19

Do you notice what number one is? Homosexuality is not even in the top seven, but a lot of the other top abominations are found rampant in the church! Within churches are lying tongues, wicked imaginations, feet running to mischief, false witnesses speaking lies, and those who spread discord among the brethren. I'm not justifying the gay lifestyle but just wondering when the church will oppose these other abominations as well in the public forum. We have to have equal weights and measures and not pick and choose between acceptable and nonacceptable abominations.

GOD'S PROMISE TO RECHAB

Now back to Jeremiah. We left him filling every bottle with wine, and now we head to the house of the Rechabites. Jeremiah was to ask them to come to one of the chambers in the house of the Lord, set wine before them, and tell them to have a drink.[9]

They absolutely refused. The Rechabites were very committed to their father's instructions. What a temptation this would be. After all, they were invited to someone else's house, even the house of the Lord. Surely they could make an exception. But oh no! Their father, Jonadab, the son of Rechab, had commanded that they could never be allowed to drink wine and they could not build a house, sow seed, or plant a vineyard. They were to dwell in tents all their days and dwell in the land where they were but sojourners. They told Jeremiah they were only in Jerusalem because the Syrian and Babylonian armies had arrived.[10]

Next the Lord wanted Jeremiah to go ask the inhabitants of Jerusalem why they wouldn't listen to Him, their Father, the way the Rechabites had been committed to their father's instructions for around the last 250 years. In our study of Jeremiah we've seen over and over again God declaring that He had risen early and spoken to them, sending all His servants the prophets, rising up early and speaking to them, asking them to please turn from their evil ways in worshipping other gods. Then in His frustration God declared that while they had not listened to or obeyed their Father, the sons of Jonadab, the son of Rechab, obeyed theirs.[11]

God then made one of the most incredible promises to the house of Rechab, telling them that just because they obeyed their father, keeping all of his commandments, they would never lack a man to stand before Him forever.[12] When we think about the comparisons between the two fathers—God and Jonadab, the son of Rechab—did Jonadab ever come close to blessing his kids as the Lord did in blessing Israel? Did their father have to continually rise up early, sending people to remind them of their obligations? Was Jonadab even around to monitor them? Jonadab was long gone, whereas the Creator of the universe was still around, watching, and had the ability to bless them for their obedience. He never came close to requiring the level of difficulty in requirements that Jonadab did.

Just who was this Jonadab, son of Rechab? He was also known as Jehonadab, as we see in the story of Jehu after he slew all the remaining house of Ahab and Jezebel.[13] It was Jehonadab who joined Jehu in the trick of bringing all those who worshipped Baal into one place. Then Jehu slew them all and destroyed all images of Baal.[14] As a matter of fact Rechab was a descendant of Moses' father-in-law, one of the Kenites.[15]

The Rechabites ended up marrying into the house of Levi. Hegesippus, who was born in about AD 110 and died in about

AD 180, wrote about the Rechabites sharing in the temple rituals down to its destruction in AD 70. He also mentioned a Rechabite priest who protested against the martyrdom of James the Just.[16]

In the twelfth century a man by the name of Benjamin of Tudela "found 100,000 Rechabite Jews, who tilled, kept flocks and herds, abstained from wine and flesh, and gave tithes to teachers who devoted themselves to studying the law and weeping for Jerusalem."[17]

Christian-history.org has an insightful article that sums it up this way:

> Somehow, perhaps because of James' strict observance of the Law, the Pharisees thought they could get him to discourage the people from believing. They asked him to stand at the pinnacle of the temple on Passover and speak. Apparently James agreed.
>
> They brought him to the top of the temple, and they shouted to him from below: "Oh, righteous one, in whom we are able to place great confidence; the people are led astray after Yeshua, the crucified one. So, declare to us, what is this way, Yeshua?"
>
> Obviously, this wasn't a very wise thing for them to do. James was ready to take full advantage of such a wonderful opportunity as this! His words are memorable: "Why do you ask me about Yeshua, the Son of Man? He sits in heaven at the right hand of the great Power, and he will soon come on the clouds of heaven!"
>
> The Pharisees were horrified, but the people loved it. They began shouting, "Hosanna to the Son of David!"
>
> The Pharisees, realizing the awful mistake they'd made, began crying out, "Oh! No! The righteous one is also in error!" You can probably guess that this had little effect on the crowd. They climbed the temple as the people shouted, reached the top, and threw James from the pinnacle of the temple, letting the people know exactly what happens to

those who dared to believe in Yeshua. Guess what? It didn't kill him. He rose to his knees and began to pray for them. "I beg of you, Lord God our Father, forgive them! They do not know what they are doing."

This would not do! The Pharisees on the ground began to stone him as he prayed, while those from the roof rushed down to join in the execution. One of the priests, however, who was a son of the Rechabites mentioned by Jeremiah the prophet, shouted, "Stop! What are you doing! The righteous one is praying for you." It was too late. A fuller (i.e., launderer) took out one of the clubs that he used to beat clothes and smashed James on the head, killing him with one blow.[18]

You can see why I love history so much. If all of us would only learn from history—or, as I have heard it said, His story!

Let's summarize some thoughts.

I find it astounding that just because the Rechabites honored their father through their obedience, God gave them the honor of having a place in the temple. So often we abuse our relationship with our heavenly Father, thinking we hold some kind of an "exemption to obedience" card that we can just pull out as needed and continue to do as we please.

QUESTIONS

- What is the Lord telling you about Himself?

- What else has the Lord taught you?

CHAPTER 10

THE FALSE PROPHETS

JEREMIAH 4-6, 8, AND 10

WANT YOU TO remember that the pharaoh of Egypt was the one who had installed Jehoiakim as king after Israel had put Jehoahaz in power, which lasted for only three months. Nebuchadnezzar then rose to power and allowed Jehoiakim to stay in power, but Jehoiakim had to become his servant, which he did for three years before he rebelled against him.[1] Nebuchadnezzar would be back! But first, it was time to send a warning for the people to repent! We are now in the last few years of Jehoiakim's reign and he is being warned again.

The Lord admonished Israel, saying that they needed to return to Him, putting their abominations out of His sight, and by so doing, they would not be moved. Jeremiah proclaimed that they needed to break up their fallow ground and quit sowing among thorns. They needed to circumcise their hearts or God's fury would come like a fire and burn to the point where no one could put out the fire because of all their evil.[2]

Jeremiah was alluding to the prophet Hosea, who had also heard this word from the Lord, saying it was time to break up their fallow ground and to start to seek the Lord so that He could rain righteousness upon them.[3] I believe this is also what Yeshua was referring to when He told the people of His day not to sow among thorns, which we understand to be speaking of not caring too much about this world or the deceitfulness of riches.[4]

Jeremiah then said it was time to blow the trumpet, to cry out to assemble themselves, and to take refuge without delay because disaster was coming from the north and great destruction! Nebuchadnezzar, the lion, had come up from his thicket, and the destroyer of nations was on his way! It was time to clothe themselves with sackcloth and lament, for the Lord had not turned back.[5]

Jeremiah was astounded at the depth of the deception of God's people who were believing in the false prophets' proclamation of peace when the sword was about to descend, reaching to the very depth of their hearts.[6] God was telling Jeremiah just how foolish His people were, because they didn't know Him and had become silly children with no understanding, who were only wise to do evil, and as far as doing good, they had no understanding.[7]

I really like what Binyamin Lau writes in his book on Jeremiah about how to tell the difference between false prophets and true prophets. One way is if the prophet is ready to pay a personal price for what he shares versus one who only prophesies what people want to hear. Another is that the true prophet must love the people and consider himself to be merely "a divine emissary whose role is to help redeem the people" and not to condemn.[8]

GOD SEEKS THOSE WHO WILL REPENT

God is always looking for righteous people and intercessors, those who understand His heart. We must remember it is the goodness of God that leads us to repentance. The wrath of God is not meant to lead us to repentance but to bring justice. As you read the Book of Revelation, you will see as God's wrath is poured out the people also stiffen their necks and refuse to repent.

If you remember, God said He would spare even Sodom if Abraham could find ten righteous. We will never know if God would have gone lower because Abraham stopped. I'm sure Abraham felt he could surely find at least ten righteous in the wicked city of Sodom. After all, there was Lot, his wife, four daughters—two married and two unmarried—and of course their two husbands, which would give him eight right there. Surely there would be at least two more!

Let's look at what the Lord told Jeremiah next. He requested that Jeremiah start running to and fro throughout the streets of Jerusalem to see if he could find anyone who executed judgment and sought the truth. If he did, God would pardon Jerusalem.[9]

This is unbelievable! Abraham was looking for ten righteous to spare Sodom, and God said He would be happy if Jeremiah could even find one among His own people, in His own city, called by His name! God was trying to figure out how He could possibly pardon the city when, after He had completely blessed them and fed them to the fullest, they turned around and committed adultery, all running to the harlot's houses, or in other words, the places of idolatry, thanking the other gods.[10]

This is why the Bible talks about blessing the Lord after we have eaten and are full so we remember who gave us the food![11] If you remember, every seventh year is a shemitah year, and the land was to rest. Then after every forty-nine years, there was to be a year of Jubilee, and the land had to rest another year.[12]

People were concerned as to what they were supposed to eat the year after Jubilee if they hadn't planted during the shemitah year or Jubilee year. (That was two years without planting any food.) God told them no faith was even required because in the sixth year of the shemitah cycle they would have triple the blessing, bringing forth food for three years![13]

Sadly they were so consumed with the blessings, they forgot and neglected the One who blessed them! One of the main reasons they went into captivity was because they had not kept the shemitah year for 490 years, which is why the captivity lasted for seventy years—so the land could catch up on its rest. For 490 years God blessed them the sixth year of the cycle with triple blessings, and in spite of it they had no time for God and just wanted to keep bringing the prosperity.

God revealed to Jeremiah that His people had been false to Him in their relationship. They were actually stating that they would have nothing to do with the Lord, believing that He didn't get involved with the affairs of man, so no evil would befall them, the sword would not come, and no famine would arise. They wrongly thought the prophets were just windbags, so God was going to make His words that come out of Jeremiah's mouth like a fire and the people like wood.[14]

The Lord was now going to bring a nation from far away to come and take everything—their produce, their flocks and herds—and destroy the walls of the towns they had put their faith in. When they asked why the Lord had done this to them, Jeremiah was to tell them that because they gave up God for strange gods in the land of Israel, they would become servants to strangers in a different land. God had given them eyes to see, but they didn't see it. He had given them ears to hear, but there was no power of hearing. God wondered why man had no fear of Him and why they were not shaking in their boots from fear when He is the

Almighty God. He is the One who put the sand as the limit for the sea as an eternal order; even though the waves are always in motion, they can't go past the limit.[15]

The root of the problem, as always, was a defiant and rebellious heart. Their hearts didn't acknowledge that the blessings came from the God of Israel. In their hearts they didn't even think that they should fear the Lord as the One who gave the rain in its seasons and gave them their appointed harvest. Sadly it goes to say that God proclaimed that among His people were found wicked men who laid in wait, setting snares to catch others.[16]

This reminds me again of the parable of the wheat and the tares. In every synagogue and in every church there are wicked people the evil one has planted to destroy from within. This goes for nations as well. The astonishing and a horrible thing to the Lord was that the prophets prophesied falsely, the priests ruled by their own power, and, above all, God said, "My people love to have it so."[17]

Jeremiah was so frustrated at that point, he wondered whom he could even speak to and give a warning, because everyone's ears were uncircumcised, which means they wouldn't listen. The word of the Lord had become a reproach to them, and they had no delight in it. We find that everyone was given to covetousness; from the prophet to the priest, everyone was dealing falsely! They were declaring peace when there was no peace. None of them were even ashamed at the abominations they were doing.[18]

THE ANCIENT PATHS

The Lord said the people needed to ask for the old paths because that is where the good way is. He told them if they walked in these ancient paths, they would find rest for their souls. But they said that there was no way they would walk there. God urgently said for them to listen to the sound of the shofar, and they said there was no way they would listen.[19]

I am reminded of when Yeshua quoted from this verse, telling all who were laboring and heavy laden to come to Him and He would give them rest. Then He stated that we should take His yoke and learn from Him, because He is gentle and lowly in heart. If we do this, we will find rest for our souls, because His yoke is easy and His burden is light.[20]

Yeshua was saying that He is the ancient path we need to walk in. He is the living Torah. Yeshua described Himself as being the way, the truth, and the life.[21] We find in Psalms that the way is where the undefiled walk and the way is walking in the Law of the Lord.[22] We also find that God's Law is the truth.[23] We also find from Proverbs that the Law is a fountain of life, the commandment is a lamp, and the Law is light.[24] Wow, Torah is the way, the truth, and the life, and as Yeshua is light, so is the Torah! Yeshua is the living Torah. We now need to hear the consequence in Jeremiah because they refused to listen to the Law. I can just hear the Lion of Judah roaring here as a shout came.

> Hear, O earth: behold, I will bring evil upon this people, even the fruit of their thoughts, because they have not hearkened unto my words, nor to my law, but rejected it.
> —JEREMIAH 6:19

The Lord questioned why the people of Jerusalem were perpetually in a backsliding condition and declared it was because they held fast to deceit and refused to return. No one would repent of their wickedness, saying they hadn't even done anything wrong. They were like horses running into battle.[25] You know how people develop muscle memory, and their actions become instinctual. In this case they are acting as animals, rushing headlong and not even stopping to think of the consequences or evaluate their actions. God made a very strong statement, saying that the stork knows her appointed times as well as the turtledove, and the crane and the swallow all know the time they are to migrate or return home, so why is it God's people did not know their appointed times? They claimed to be wise and that the Lord was with them. The problem was they claimed to be wise, but they had rejected the word of the Lord. So what wisdom did they really have?[26] Therefore He would give their wives and fields to others because every one of them was given to covetousness; everyone from the prophet to the priest dealt falsely, proclaiming peace when there was no peace.[27]

Israel has always wanted to assimilate and be like all the other nations. Yet God wants them to be separate. Today God still wants His people to be separate. The Lord told them not to learn the way of the heathen, being dismayed at the signs in the heavens. He also didn't want them to follow the customs of the heathen in cutting a tree down out of the forest, bringing it home, and then decorating it with silver and gold after fastening it with a hammer and nails so it doesn't fall.[28] Talk about an old pagan tradition! A great commotion was coming out of the north country to make the cities of Judah desolate.[29] Prepare the way!

As we all know, even President Trump is trying to bring peace to the Middle East. He would love to be the one to make the deal! Let me tell you right now, there will be no peace in the Middle East until Messiah comes. There is a big difference between a peacekeeper and a peacemaker. A peacekeeper has to keep two people from killing each other, whereas a peacemaker resolves the conflict and can leave. Islam can never allow Israel to claim ownership of any part of the land of Israel. It has not been, nor will it ever be, a real estate issue. It is a religious issue. If Israel wins, Allah loses, and Islam cannot allow that. Any peace agreement that divides the land of Israel or Jerusalem, creating a

Palestinian capital or state, is what will bring about God's wrath upon the nations that participated in dividing it, as the Bible states in Joel 3:1–2.

Let's summarize some thoughts.

There were mostly false prophets in Jeremiah's day, much like what is in the church today. They either prophesy lies, saying what the people want to hear and declaring that all is well—"Peace, peace; when there is no peace"[30]—or at the other extreme they prophesy out of personal anger, hitting people over the head with their own personal version of the wrath of God.

The true prophets will keep themselves out of the picture and only express God's words and feelings as a loving Father trying to correct His wayward children. There is far too much "personal prophecy" in the church, where these so-called prophets actually are just trying to draw people unto themselves.

I also found it amazing that God had blessed His children with three years of produce in one year just so they could spend a two-year vacation with Him, and they refused. They accepted the blessing and then went on with work, not wanting to spend any time with their Creator. The people also claimed to be wise, but they threw out the Torah, thinking they knew better.

Questions

- What is the Lord telling you about Himself?

- What else has the Lord taught you?

CHAPTER 11

WAYWARD PRIESTS AND PROPHETS

JEREMIAH 23

W E NOW COME to the final chapter of Jehoiakim's reign. There came a warning of woe to the pastors/shepherds that were destroying and scattering the sheep of God's pasture. Though they had scattered and driven away His flock, God would gather the remnant out of all the countries where they were driven, bring them back to their folds, and set up pastors who would feed them and not fleece them so they will not be in fear or lacking anything.[1] God said He would raise up a righteous Branch, a king who would reign and execute judgment and justice in the earth, and when He reigned, Judah would be saved, and Israel would dwell safely. His name would be "THE LORD OUR RIGHTEOUSNESS."[2]

Here we find the Lord again declared a coming event that would be so amazing that it would eclipse the original exodus from Egypt. God declared He would bring the children of Israel out of all the countries that they had been scattered to, back to the land that He promised them.[3] I believe this began to happen in part at the end of the nineteenth century, but to me, this prophecy seems to foretell of an exodus from all the nations back to Israel about as large and quick as the original exodus.

Jeremiah then revealed just how broken his own heart was because of all the false prophets. His bones were shaking so badly that he likened himself to a drunk, all because of the staggering thoughts of God's holiness and His land being full of adulterers, swearing, profane prophets and priests, and wickedness in the very house of the Lord! The time of their visitation was coming![4]

DISCERNING THE TIMES

As we know, history repeats itself, and we find Yeshua told the people of Jerusalem that once again their enemies would surround them and level them to the ground, all because they did not know the time of their visitation.[5] God wants you to know how to tell what the biblical time is!

To my dismay, many believers do not know how to tell biblical time. We do know that "to every thing there is a season, and a time to every purpose under heaven...a time to plant, and a time to pluck up that which is planted."[6] God informed Jeremiah that for him it was plucking time. Today, though, many are planting at plucking time and plucking at planting time. This is why the church needs to get on the biblical calendar to know what God is doing so we can work beside Him. The Bible asks if two can walk together unless they are in agreement.[7] Do you want to walk with God? Then you need to know His appointed times.

Many churches celebrate the resurrection of Messiah an entire month before He even died on Passover because the church decided the Bible was in error in giving the Jews the opportunity to celebrate Passover twice in the same year if they missed the first opportunity for specific reasons. The church determined that in no way should they follow the biblical calendar due to their anti-Semitism, and they changed the way to determine the biblical calendar back in the fourth century. Instead of following the Bible, they went by their reason and approved what the majority wanted.

Religious leaders, many times, are the tares planted within the church. The Lord professed that He had seen the prophets of Jerusalem doing horrible things, such as committing adultery, walking in lies, and strengthening the hand of evildoers. None of them returned from their wickedness. All of them were as Sodom and Gomorrah to the Lord.[8]

Last year I spoke at a church in Houston, Texas, and took an Uber to the airport. A very sweet lady was my driver, and we got to talking about the Bible. I perceived from our conversation that she was a very religious Catholic, and we had a great hour-long conversation to the airport. Being raised in a very religious Catholic family myself, I understood where she was coming from. I told her how I had left Catholicism, and I knew she was secretly rooting for me to come back.

I ended up giving her one of my books, and she handed me a book that she wanted me to read: *Letter to a Suffering Church* by Bishop Robert Barron. It speaks about the sexual abuse crisis and why Catholics should stay Catholic, even with so much scandal going on. I found the book fascinating for several reasons, but let me share with you a couple of things. We know sexual abuse exists within the religious community, both Catholic and Protestant, and even in Pentecostal churches as well as synagogues. In the book Barron mentions that there was a group of priests in the Pittsburgh diocese that actually acted as a predatory ring, identifying potential candidates for abuse and passing the information about them back and forth to each other.[9] He mentions a pope in the early sixteenth century known as Alexander VI. He had a string of mistresses with whom he fathered at least ten illegitimate children.[10]

It is unbelievable, yet tares have been among the wheat for thousands of years. The morals of the church have fallen below the standard of the world from just eighty years ago. God is watching and keeping record, and judgment day is coming.

In Jeremiah, God had determined a whirlwind was coming forth in great fury that would fall grievously on the head of the wicked. The anger of the Lord was not going to return until He had executed and performed the thoughts of His heart.[11]

I find it interesting that it says that "in the latter days ye shall consider it perfectly."[12] We are definitely in the latter days. This reminds me of the verse in Isaiah that states the word of the Lord will not return void, but it will accomplish what He purposed.[13]

The false prophets were on the run where God never sent them, and God was wondering why they didn't at least wait to hear His counsel. Maybe, just maybe, the people might have repented.[14] How often do people think they can hide what they do from God? The Bible says that men's hearts are fully set to do evil when the punishment is delayed.[15]

So many believe that because the Lord is patient in bringing judgement, He is clueless or uninterested—we read earlier that this was the very thought of the people. Now we find the Lord was declaring that no one would be able to hide themselves in any secret place where He wouldn't be seen, as He fills heaven and earth. He sees and hears it all! The Lord declared He had heard what the prophets had been saying, prophesying lies, and in His name saying they had a prophetic dream. These prophets were actually trying to use their made-up dreams to make people forget God's name and exchange it for Baal.[16]

I find it very interesting that there is a verse in the Song of Songs about the bride trying to hide in secret places when the groom was calling to please come out from hiding so he could see her, and they could go care for his vineyard. He told her it was because the foxes were destroying the vines.[17] We know Israel is the vine, and Ezekiel told us who the foxes were—the false prophets![18]

When God does give a word, the prophet must speak faithfully the word or dream that he or she is given! God's word is compared to a fire or a hammer that breaks rocks into pieces! This is why the Lord went on to say that He was against the prophets who were stealing His words and the prophets who prophesied false dreams.[19] The Lord told Jeremiah that when anyone—be it prophet, priest, or commoner—asked him what the burden of the Lord was, he was to respond with, "What burden, I will even forsake you!"[20]

It's as if the people were pretending that they really cared when they actually couldn't have cared less. They inquired what the Lord's burden was as if they wanted to help relieve it. How absurd. God declared that they had "perverted the words of the living God."[21] Because they repeated their meaningless inquiry, the Lord would forget them, cast them out of His presence, and bring perpetual reproach and shame upon them that would never be forgotten.[22]

As we wrap up the eleven-year reign of Jehoiakim, we will research what the Scriptures reveal from different sources, starting with 2 Kings 24. We discover that Jehoiakim's son

Jehoiachin reigned in his stead. If you remember, Josiah had more than one wife, and after Israel installed Jehoahaz, Egypt hauled him off and installed his half-brother Jehoiakim, to the delight of his mother, I'm sure. Jehoiakim was beholden to Nebuchadnezzar because he had temporarily subdued Egypt.[23]

It is breathtaking as we see what unfolds in the upcoming events. You have to remember that in the third year of Jehoiakim, Nebuchadnezzar besieged Jerusalem and took captives to Babylon.[24] The fourth year of Jehoiakim was the first full year of Nebuchadnezzar's reign.[25] The fifth year of Jehoiakim was the second year of Nebuchadnezzar, when the three Hebrew children were thrown into the fiery furnace. So Jehoiakim served Nebuchadnezzar three years, and then he rebelled against him.[26]

So Nebuchadnezzar returned to Jerusalem and besieged it again. Nebuchadnezzar then hauled Jehoiakim in fetters to Babylon, just as Pharaoh had hauled Jehoahaz to Egypt. Israel then decided to appoint Jehoiakim's son Jehoiachin to be king. But just as with Egypt, Nebuchadnezzar came back a few months later and said forget this. He deposed Jehoiachin after only three months and installed the younger brother of his half-uncle Jehoahaz, who had been hauled off to Egypt, and now it was Zedekiah who was beholden to Babylon!

So Nebuchadnezzar hauled Jehoiachin, his mother, his servants, and his leaders to Babylon, along with all the treasures from the house of the Lord and the king's house.[27] This was all done according to word of the Lord through Isaiah to Hezekiah! He also carried off ten thousand captives, of which seven thousand were mighty men of war, along with a thousand craftsman and smiths, leaving but the poor of the land. He then made Mattaniah king and changed his name to Zedekiah.[28]

In Chronicles the Bible says that Jehoiachin was eight years old when he began to reign, reigning three months and ten days.[29]

But in Kings it says Jehoiachin was eighteen when he began to reign and reigned three months.[30] So which is right? I believe the answer is both! When Jehoiakim began to reign in his second year, his son was eight years old and was made coregent along with dad to assure the kingship would fall to him rather than going back to Zedekiah, who was older. God had different ideas, so when his actual reign began at eighteen, off he went to Babylon.

The end of Jeremiah summarizes the different times of the various captivities, and we find that, besides the one in the third year of Jehoiakim mentioned in the first chapter of Daniel, in the seventh year of Nebuchadnezzar, which is the tenth year of Jehoiakim, 3,023 captives were taken.[31] The following year ten thousand captives were taken to Babylon in the next wave, as we have just read.

Just who was taken in this wave to Babylon with King Jehoiachin and his mother? For that we go to the Book of Esther! We find out from the second chapter of the Book of Esther that this was when Mordecai was taken into captivity.[32]

Let's do some dating. The temple was destroyed in 587 or 586 BC, and whichever you believe is fine with me. If you say it was 587 BC, and you remember Zedekiah reigned for eleven years and then the temple was destroyed, that would put this captivity of Jehoiachin at the beginning of Zedekiah's reign eleven years earlier, which would be 598 BC.

Amazingly, sources date the story of Esther as occurring during the rule of Ahasuerus, beginning around 483 BC and ending around 473 BC. Some date it even much later. Let's stay with the earliest sources and try to figure out how old Mordecai was when he refused to bow down to Haman. Let's say he was only ten years old when he was taken in 598 BC. Let's say the event when Mordecai refused to bow to Haman happened in the seventh year of Ahasuerus' reign, based on the scripture that says Esther was picked in the seventh year of his reign.[33]

Now for some math: 483 BC minus seven years equals 476 BC. If we take 598 BC, when they were taken to Babylon, down to 476 BC, the seventh year of Ahasuerus' reign, we get 122 years. Adding that Mordecai may have been ten years old when he was taken into captivity in 598 BC, that would make Mordecai 132 years old at the time he refused to bow! We even discover from the Book of Ezra that when the remnant that was carried away to Babylon finally returned to Jerusalem after the seventy-year captivity, Mordecai was among those who returned![34]

If we go back to Jeremiah chapter 52, we see in the eighteenth year of Nebuchadnezzar, which would be exactly 587 BC, when the temple was destroyed, we find that 832 more people were taken captive.[35] Five years later, in 582 BC, the twenty-third year of Nebuchadnezzar, Nebuzaradan, the captain of the guard, took another 745 people. Then Jeremiah stated that all the people were 4,600.[36]

Let's summarize some thoughts.

God's greatest angst has always been with the religious leaders, be they pastors, priests, or prophets. They often become more concerned with what tradition says than with what God says. They either fear their denominational leaders or fear their flock, worried about losing their jobs if they go against their denominational tradition. Believers need to get on God's calendar so they won't miss the time of God's next visitation!

Questions

- What is the Lord telling you about Himself?

- What else has the Lord taught you?

CHAPTER 12

A NEW COVENANT

JEREMIAH 30–31, 24, AND 29

As Zedekiah's reign began, the Lord told Jeremiah to write all the words He had spoken to him in a book for himself because the days were coming that He would bring back all the captives of His people Israel and Judah and cause them to return to the land of their fathers and possess it.[1] This referred to the land promised to their fathers, not Argentina and not the United States!

We now come to a famous reference concerning the time of Jacob's trouble. In Christianity this is thought of as the great tribulation. God questioned the reason why all the men acted as though they were in labor with a child and why every man's face turned pale.[2] This is what Yeshua referenced as well when He spoke of these times being as birth pangs.[3]

Fortunately Israel will be saved out of all this. So God declared for Jacob not to fear and for Israel not to be dismayed because He would save them from afar! The time was coming when no one would make Israel afraid, and God said that although He would make an end of all the other nations where He scattered them, He would not completely make an end of them. They wouldn't go unpunished, but God would correct them in justice.[4]

There was a warning here that God would devour all the nations who devoured the Jewish people, who, along with all their foes, would be going into captivity. All who plundered Israel would be plundered, and everyone who preyed on the Jewish people, God would make prey. God declared He would restore all the fortunes of Israel, producing songs of thanksgiving.[5]

He then informed Israel that His wrath would be as a tornado on the head of the wicked, He would not stop until He accomplished all His intentions, and this would be fully understood in the latter days.[6]

When this happened, God declared that He would be the God of all the families of Israel, and they were going to be His people. The Lord appeared and began to woo Israel back by explaining that He had loved them with an everlasting love, and with lovingkindness He would draw them back to Himself. God wanted Israel to know that He would rebuild their nation, and they would plant vineyards on the mountains of Samaria again. The day would come when the watchmen on Mount Ephraim would cry out when it was time to go up to Mount Zion where the Lord our God is![7]

A point to be considered about this new covenant coming: If you remember, Ephraim, or Israel, and Judah had been at odds and even in a civil war. Going back to even earlier generations, the separation came from Jeroboam not wanting the northern tribes to go to Jerusalem for the festivals, so he created altars in Bethel and Dan for the people to go to. Now in Jeremiah 31, we are told of those in Samaria planting vineyards and coming up to Zion, proclaiming that Jerusalem is where the Lord is! Interestingly the Hebrew word for *watchmen* in Jeremiah 31:6 is *notzrim*, which today is the word used to refer to Christians.

This verse has great prophetic implications. Right now Samaria is considered the West Bank and is to be a part of a created Palestinian state. This verse declares that Samaria will be in Israel's hands! This prophecy is being fulfilled even now as there are Christian groups in Samaria who help plant and harvest vineyards for the Jewish people, and many Gentile Christians are becoming ardent Zionists, wanting to go up to Zion and keep the feasts!

The fullness of the Gentiles is arriving. The word *fullness* does not refer to a quantity but maturity. You don't complete harvest when the crop is not mature. God will not marry a child bride but rather a mature bride. He is waiting for the fullness of the Gentiles, or I could say He is waiting for the church to grow up and mature. Too many churches keep their members in diapers, only feeding them milk and not meat. We also see the maturity of the Gentiles will come when they realize it is not about them and they desire to go up to Zion. After the fullness of the Gentiles comes, the fullness of the Jews will come, when they too will become Zionists and want to build the temple.

There will then be a cry for God to save His people, and He will bring them from the north country and even from the ends of the earth, with a great company returning. God told all the nations to listen up, as He who scattered Israel will also gather her and protect her as a shepherd does his flock. The Lord has redeemed and ransomed Jacob from the one who was stronger.[8] His people will come singing and rejoicing for all the blessings, and they will turn their mourning into joy.[9]

Why were they mourning? We hear of a prophetic voice being heard in Ramah of wailing and bitter weeping. It was Rachel, weeping for her children, for her sons. She refused to be comforted for her sons because they were gone.[10] Rachel's tomb is in Bethlehem, and I have visited it several times. The Gospel of Matthew tells us when Herod slew all the baby boys two years old and younger in Bethlehem, this prophecy was fulfilled.[11]

In Jeremiah it goes on to say for them to hold back all the tears because they would all come back from the land of the enemy, and there was a hope for the future, that their sons would be back. We hear of Ephraim repenting and the Lord declaring that He would have mercy on him as well.[12]

Shedding Light on an Important Scripture

Fasten your seatbelts now, as I am going to share with you something very amazing about a Scripture verse. This comes to me from one of my great friends, Rabbi Itzhak Shapira, founder of Ahavat Ammi Ministries and the author of the book *Return of the Kosher Pig*. Here's the verse:

> Is Ephraim my dear son? is he a pleasant child?
> —JEREMIAH 31:20

In some Bibles this is verse 19. Rabbi Shapira points out there are two different Hebrew words used for *son* and *child*. The word for *son* is *ben*, and the word for *child* is *yeled*. A child, or a yeled, refers to one who is lowly and humble. A son, or a ben, refers to rulership, as in the Son of Man or the Son of David.

> For unto us a child is born, unto us a son is given: and the government shall be upon his shoulder: and his name shall be called Wonderful, Counsellor, The mighty God, The everlasting Father, The Prince of Peace. Of the increase of

> his government and peace there shall be no end, upon the
> throne of David, and upon his kingdom, to order it, and to
> establish it with judgment and with justice from henceforth
> even for ever.
>
> —Isaiah 9:6–7

We know this refers to the Messiah and not Hezekiah, as some believe, because of the titles such as mighty God, everlasting Father, etc. But notice the order, where now the word *child*, or *yeled*, comes first and then son, or *ben*, comes second. The yeled represents Messiah's first coming, humble and lowly, riding on a donkey. His second coming will be as the Son of God, ruling on the throne of David! Daniel saw this when in the night visions he saw the Son of Man coming with the clouds of heaven, and to Him was given dominion, glory, and a kingdom, that all nations would serve Him.[13]

Most religious Jews see two Messiahs coming: one is the son of Joseph, who is a suffering servant, and the other is the son of David, coming as a conquering King. Isaiah spoke of one person who accomplishes both! Ezekiel spoke of two sticks coming together as one. One is for Joseph, and one is for Judah.[14] The two branches becoming one could mean the understanding of the Messiah coming from the two main houses of Israel, but they really represented that there is only one Messiah, who comes two times. And the time is coming when that will be realized, and then the new covenant with both houses really will take off!

Just as God had promised to pluck the people up, as we read earlier, God now promised He would plant them back again.[15] One of the promises I love most confirms this. It is in the Book of Amos, where the Lord stated He would plant them upon their land, and they would never be plucked up again from the Promised Land He gave them.[16] The key is to set up the waymarks and make signposts so the way back can be clearly found.[17] The waymarks refer to the way to Zion!

Then came one of the greatest promises in the Bible. God promised to cut a new covenant.[18] In Christianity the new covenant is a big deal. But I have to point out that the new covenant is a covenant made with Judah and Israel and not with Gentiles or non-Jews. If you get rid of your old car and get a new car, it is your car. If my old car is sent off to the dump, it doesn't mean my neighbor gets a new car; I get the new car.

For Gentiles to participate in the new covenant given to Israel and Judah, we need to be grafted in. God did not plant a separate Gentile tree in Rome. The tree stayed in Jerusalem, and we are grafted into the tree of Israel with all those who have circumcised hearts. We are grafted into the same tree made up of all those Jews of faith mentioned in the Book of Hebrews, chapter 11.

The new covenant, the passage also said, is not throwing out all the laws of God but having them all written on our hearts. And when that happens, we will be the people of God.[19] Ezekiel explained it as if we were getting a heart transplant. God will not only put a new heart in us but a new spirit as well. He will put His Spirit in us to enable us to faithfully walk in His statutes.[20] This is not to be done out of fear or obligation but out of love.

The Lord said that He would forgive their iniquity and wouldn't remember the sins of Israel. He went on to say that the only way Israel would cease being a nation before Him would be when the sun, moon, and stars don't exist anymore and the waves of the sea stop roaring. Then He added that as soon as one of us humans can measure the heavens above or search out the foundations of the earth, then He will cast off Israel for all they have done.[21]

Zedekiah's Reign Begins

Zedekiah was twenty-one years old when he began to reign, and he reigned eleven years in Jerusalem. He only did evil, never humbled himself before Jeremiah, and even rebelled against Nebuchadnezzar, who made him swear by God. Instead he stiffened his neck and hardened his heart against God.[22]

We find that the chief priests and the people transgressed very greatly following after the abominations of the nations. They even polluted the house of the Lord after God sent them His messengers because He had compassion on both them and His dwelling place.[23] Chronicles states that after He showed them compassion by sending His messengers, they mocked them, despised His words, and scoffed at His prophets, until God's wrath rose against them.[24]

This reminds me of a parable in the Gospel of Matthew in which a householder took great care planting a vineyard and let it out to husbandmen. When the harvest came, he sent his servants to receive the fruit. They took the servants and beat one, killed one, and stoned another. Finally he sent his son, and they killed him as well.[25] History continues to repeat itself.

The Lord allowed Jeremiah to see two baskets of figs that were set before the temple after Nebuchadnezzar had hauled off Jeconiah with his mother and thousands of others. One basket of figs looked wonderful, and the other was filled with figs so rotten that they couldn't even be eaten. God explained that the basket of good figs represented those who had been exiled to Babylon for their benefit, and He would bring them back again to Israel and replant them because they were returning to Him with all their hearts. As for the bad figs that were putrid, they would be given to all those who remained in the land of Israel and those who dwelled in Egypt, making them a horror and a curse, sending them the sword and famine until they were destroyed from the land of Israel.[26]

Jeremiah decided to write a letter to all the exiles whom Nebuchadnezzar had taken to Babylon.[27] There is always a remnant left in the land, and in this case Shaphan and Hilkiah were a few of them. If you remember, Hilkiah found the Torah scroll back in King Josiah's day and gave it to the scribe Shaphan, who read it before the king, and the king repented and rent his clothes.

Shaphan had a son named Elasah, and he and Hilkiah's son Gemariah were picked by Zedekiah to deliver the scroll containing the words of Jeremiah to the captives. He told them to build houses and live in them, plant gardens and eat of the fruit, take wives for their sons and give their daughters to husbands that they might multiply, and pray for peace because they weren't going anywhere for a while.[28]

While they were there, they were not to let the false prophets and fortune tellers in their midst deceive them. They were only prophesying falsely in God's name because He had not sent them. Jeremiah then gave them the bad news that seventy years had been allotted for them to be in Babylon. But he also comforted them by letting them know that God had a purpose for them, and it was for peace and not for evil, giving them a future and a hope. It was while they were in exile they were to call upon the Lord and pray, and God would listen to them. They were exhorted to seek God because they would find Him when they sought Him with all their hearts.[29]

I don't know how many of you played hide-and-seek growing up, but I loved it. I loved the hunt, and I loved the hiding. I can remember some of us hiding so well that people gave up searching. The game was over, and we were still hiding, not knowing everyone had stopped searching.

I believe God also loves to play hide and seek. He loves to search for us, and He is disappointed when we stop searching for Him. The reason He hides, I believe, is to see how strong our desire is to find Him. There is a heart that seeks God, and then there is heart that is desperately seeking God. We need to be desperately seeking for God, and not out of some need but out of a desire to know Him!

I will never forget one of the many airline experiences I have had. If you travel by plane, you know that as soon as the door chime dings at the arrival gate, people immediately stand up, get their luggage, and are as anxious as a herd of cats to get out of there. The aisle is completely blocked with luggage and passengers waiting to disembark. Everyone is jumping on their phones, making contact with someone.

Well, there was this lady next to me who got on her phone. I could easily hear the conversation, especially when she raised her voice because she was talking to the lady who had been watching her kids while she was gone. The lady who was supposed to be watching her kids told her that her kids didn't come home, and she had no idea where they were. This woman's eyes got so big. She got totally lit up and ready to bolt to find her kids, even though she was at the back of a plane with the aisle filled with people.

That moment I saw what true passion and desire was in seeking a loved one. There was no stopping her. Katie, bar the door! She was leaping over seats, weaving in and out, yelling, "Get out of my way!"

God is looking to see how strong our desire is to find Him. The Bible concept of the phrase *believe in God* really means to trust in Him. While many ask whether people believe in God, the real question is, Do they trust God? During the exodus, all the people knew God existed, but the real question was, Did they believe in Him or trust Him? The question I like to ask is, Does God believe in you and me? Can God trust us enough to give us the responsibility of being a good witness for His kingdom?

In Jeremiah 29:15–32 we find the Jews in Babylon were not seeking the Lord, and they were proclaiming that the Lord had raised up prophets in Babylon who were telling them they would soon return. So the Lord said He was going to send them the sword, famine, and plague and make them like the worthless figs that couldn't be eaten because they were so bad. All of this was because they would not listen to His words.

To those in captivity in Babylon the Lord proclaimed that He was going to send a couple of false prophets in Jerusalem to Babylon, and they would be slain before them.[30] Then the word of the Lord came to Jeremiah concerning a specific false prophet in Babylon who was also prophesying lies. God said he would be punished for teaching rebellion against the Lord.[31]

Let's summarize some thoughts.

Restoration is still available after we sin, thank God! There is a new covenant coming for Israel and Judah, and non-Jews are able to be grafted into it along with the Jewish people. We saw how God will never forsake the Jewish people, and the only way they would disappear would be if the sun, moon, and stars disappear. In spite of all these blessings and the mercy God showed, we continue to see that His children often remain stiff-necked. There are so many false prophets out there speaking falsehoods in the Lord's name that it is truly scary how many people are deceived and believe them. We need to have the heart of that mother on the crowded plane. "I am going after God, and nothing is stopping me!" You might enjoy going to the Book of Ezekiel and seeing what was going on over there at this time.

QUESTIONS

- What is the Lord telling you about Himself?

- What else has the Lord taught you?

CHAPTER 13

WARNINGS TO THE NATIONS

JEREMIAH 46–51

W E ARE NOW in the first three years of Zedekiah's reign when the Lord gave Jeremiah warnings to deliver to the other nations, beginning with Egypt. God warned them to get ready to fight because Nebuchadnezzar was coming! He was coming on a day of vengeance to avenge God on His adversaries.[1] The Lord proclaimed destruction on specific cities in Egypt—Migdol, Noph, and Tahpanhes—and you will see it is because the Jewish people would flee to these cities in the future. If you remember, Egypt went through Israel to help Assyria fight Babylon. They fled in fear back to Egypt. They cried out that Pharaoh was nothing but a windbag.[2]

Historically it was in 605 BC that Nebuchadnezzar defeated the Egyptian forces at Carchemish. Four years later they fought to a stalemate at the Egyptian border. God then told Egypt that they better prepare to go into captivity. He would bring punishment on their cities, pharaoh, and all their gods, and they would be delivered into Babylon's hands. As for Israel, they were told not to fear because God would eventually save them from afar. Their offspring would return to the Promised Land, and God would be with them—but then it would be the time to make a complete end of all the other nations.[3]

After God's warning to Egypt, we move on to His warning to the Philistines. He warned them that Nebuchadnezzar would be coming their way as well. In the very near future all their inhabitants and even the men would cry out and wail because of the noise from the stomping horses, rushing chariots, and rumbling wheels. I can see it now! He warned them that fathers wouldn't even look back for their children because they would lack the courage. All of the allies of the Philistines would be cut off as well.[4]

Starting from the west coast, the Lord then moved to the east, warning Moab and declaring a woe to Nebo.[5] If you remember, Moses' last stand was at Nebo, where he was given an opportunity to look into the Promised Land right before he died.[6] The woe against Moab came because they had trusted in their own works and their own treasures.[7] Remember that Moab came from Lot, Abraham's nephew.[8] The Moabites served the god Chemosh, to whom they would sacrifice their children by throwing them into the fire.

Within this curse given to Moab, we find that one is cursed when he does the work of the Lord deceitfully.[9] This reminds me of a pastor in Wichita, Kansas, where I lived back in the '70s, who was convicted of funneling drug money through his church. We know the heart is desperately wicked and able to deceive its owner.

The Gospel of Matthew describes that there will be *many* who ask the Lord to let them into the kingdom of heaven because in His name they had prophesied, cast out devils, and done many wonderful works. But He will tell them to get lost, as they are just workers of iniquity![10] We have just been reading about false prophets who love to name-drop God's name. There are only three major monotheistic religions in the world: Judaism, Christianity, and Islam. Who do you think this prophecy from Matthew is referring to? How many Jews or Muslims cast out demons, prophesy, or do wonderful works, proclaiming the name of Jesus? It doesn't happen, so who else could this be speaking to?

Because the Moabites had exalted themselves against the Lord, they would get to wallow in their own vomit. Moab was exceedingly proud, arrogant, and haughty. They believed that lying would make everything right.[11]

The Lord then turned to the Ammonites, who were Moab's brothers to the north, where Reuben, Gad, and the half-tribe of Manasseh had dwelled. He asked the Ammonites why their god Milcom[12] should inherit the land belonging to Gad and his people should get to dwell there. The Lord said that their place would be burnt to the ground and Israel would again take possession of it.[13]

The whole problem in the Middle East has always been a religious problem. I once saw a bumper sticker that read, "My god can beat up your god." The whole boiling point in the Middle East regarding a two-state solution in Israel is that all the wise men of the earth don't recognize the problem. Muslim fanatics can't handle that Israel's God has retaken the territory that belonged at one time to their god and his people. Islamic radicals can never accept a two-state solution; their goal is only one state, with all the Jews cast into the sea.

Next came the woe against Edom—representing Esau, who was Jacob's brother—which was to the south of Moab. God said the inhabitants of their land would have the calamity of Esau brought down upon them when they were punished.[14] Bozrah would become a desolation and its cities a perpetual waste. Edom also was full of pride, and God said though they had made their nest as the stars, they were coming down! Edom would also be an astonishment and end up like Sodom and Gomorrah, where no one would ever be able to live.[15]

Isaiah mentioned Edom's destruction as well when he wondered who was coming from Edom with dyed garments from Bozrah. He was glorious in His apparel, and Isaiah was wondering why the garments were all red, as if He had been treading in a winepress. The answer came when the One dressed in the apparel explained that He had been treading the winepress alone and no one else was with Him. He had trampled the inhabitants in His wrath, with their lifeblood spattered on His garments as the day of vengeance and the year of redemption had come.[16]

An End-Times Connection

There is a huge biblical connection here to the last days. History always repeats itself, but from different angles with different players. We need to look for patterns. We know from the Book of Revelation that the apostle John saw heaven opened and One on a white horse about to make war, and His garments were dipped in blood. His name was called the Word of God. Behind Him, His armies rode on white horses, clothed in clean white linen, and it says that He treads the winepress of the fierceness and wrath of Almighty God![17]

Christians believe this speaks of Yeshua. A connection needs to be made between this event and Yom Kippur. Yeshua, as the High Priest, when He comes to make war on earth, will not be wearing a Roman soldier costume; He will be wearing white linen.

We know from Revelation that white linen represents the righteousness of the saints. Everyone wears white on Yom Kippur, the Day of Atonement, and Revelation describes an event that will take place some year on Yom Kippur. Here are some fascinating parallels that further explain the connection between this event when Yeshua comes on the white horse with all the saints in white and the day of Yom Kippur.

We read that He tread the winepress all alone, which correlates to the fact that during the Yom Kippur service, no man can enter the tabernacle when the high priest goes into the holy of holies, where the ark of the covenant is, to make atonement for Israel. The high priest is sprinkling blood everywhere, and you can imagine all the blood splashing on his white linen garments.[18]

In Revelation, when John saw the temple of the tabernacle being opened in heaven, the angels came out dressed in white linen. The temple was filled with smoke, and no one was able to enter the temple till the seven plagues were fulfilled.[19] We have to remember that when God showed Moses the pattern to build the tabernacle, it was based on a heavenly pattern. What was to happen on earth was to echo what was happening in the heavenlies. So the tabernacle on earth was patterned after the one in heaven. Yom Kippur is the day of judgment when God's justice will prevail on earth.

We also find when the seventh angel sounded the trumpet, the nations were angry that they should be judged and God's servants would be rewarded. The temple of God was opened in heaven, and the true ark was seen.[20] The ark is only able to be seen at Yom Kippur!

In Leviticus the high priest is told to take a censer of burning coals from the altar before the Lord, having his hands full of sweet incense to put on the fire, causing a great cloud of incense to cover the mercy seat.[21] We know incense speaks of the prayers of the saints.[22] What do we find in Revelation but the Yom Kippur service in action? We have an angel with a golden censer, and to him was given much incense to be offered with the prayers of the saints on the golden altar which was before the throne. The smoke of the incense came with the prayers of the saints ascending before God. The angel then took fire from the altar and cast it to the earth.[23]

We find that much of the Book of Revelation was patterned after the feasts of Israel, and the events foretold in John's Revelation will happen on those feast days, but we do not know what year. If Messiah fulfilled the spring feasts to the day of His first coming, He will also fulfill the fall feasts to the day of His second coming! (This is a good reason to be on God's calendar, the Hebrew calendar, instead of the pagan one.)

Next came the Word of the Lord to Babylon, and we can see a lot more connections with the Book of Revelation. Jeremiah declared that Babylon was done for.[24] When this happened, the children of Israel would come with the children of Judah to seek the Lord their God. They were going to ask the way to Zion and join themselves to the Lord in a perpetual covenant that would never be forgotten. The Lord proclaimed that His people had been lost sheep because the shepherds were the ones who led them astray, causing them to forget their resting place. Sadly those who found the lost sheep of Israel devoured them, and—get a load of this!—the adversaries who devoured them made a statement that what they had done in devouring them was not offensive because they had sinned against the Lord![25] This has been the very statement from many of the early church fathers.

St. Jerome (AD 347–420) describes the Jews as "serpents wearing the image of Judas. Their psalms and prayers are the braying of donkeys."[26]

At the end of the fourth century the bishop of Antioch, John Chrysostom, a great orator, wrote a series of eight sermons against the Jews. To quote him: "the synagogue is not only a brothel and a theater; it is also a den of robbers and a lodging for wild beasts. No Jew adores God…Jews are inveterate murderers, possessed by the devil, their debauchery and drunkenness gives them the manners of the pig."[27]

In the fifth century the burning question was, If the Jews and Judaism were cursed by God, then how can you explain their continued existence? Augustine confronted this problem in his "Sermon Against the Jews." He maintained that the Jews deserved the most severe punishment for having "killed our Jesus"[28] and that they have only been kept alive by divine providence to serve, together with their Scriptures, as witness to the truth of Christianity.

In the Book of Revelation the people were on the way to Zion to join themselves to the Lord, and we hear of a Lamb standing on Mount Zion with 144,000 who have His Father's name written on their foreheads.[29] Who were these 144,000? We find they were 12,000 from every tribe of Israel.[30] Along with them came a great multitude that no one could number from all the other nations, kindreds, and tongues. They were also clothed in white robes with palms in their hands.[31]

In Jeremiah, concerning Babylon, it was prophesied that a great assembly of nations would come against her. Their arrows would be as a mighty expert man with none returning in vain.[32] The Hebrew word here describing the arrows is a word that means smart or intelligent. Can you believe that? During the 1991 war with Iraq (modern-day Babylon), a great assembly of nations came against Saddam Hussein, and the missiles shot were very "smart" in the way they could be adjusted to hit their targets.

We find Isaiah prophesied the downfall of Babylon as well, beginning with a claim of having birth pangs like a woman in travail. He was in so much pain he couldn't even hear or see. A watchman he placed on the wall reported that Babylon had fallen and all the graven images were cast to the ground.[33]

Jeremiah declared that Babylon's foundations had fallen, and her walls had been thrown down as it was the day of vengeance.[34] In Revelation an angel proclaimed that Babylon had fallen because she made all nations drink of the wine of wrath because of her fornication.[35] We also read of another crying with a loud voice that Babylon the great had fallen and had become the habitation of devils.[36]

Israel was described in Jeremiah as scattered sheep that the lions had driven away, referring to Assyria and the first captivity, and now Nebuchadnezzar had broken their bones. So God declared He would punish the king of Babylon and his land just as He punished Assyria. He said that, at that time, the iniquity of Israel would be sought for and there would be none. The same with the sins of Judah—they wouldn't be found because God would pardon them.[37] Just as the Pharaoh of Egypt was refusing to let Israel go, the nations that took them captive also refused to let them go.

But the Scripture says that their Redeemer is strong! Their redeemer is the Lord of Hosts, who will plead their cause.[38] God proclaimed He would overthrow Babylon like Sodom and Gomorrah, and pangs like a woman in travail would overtake its king![39]

Israel had not been forsaken by the Lord, nor had Judah—even though their land was filled with sin against the Holy One of Israel. Why? Because God was in covenant with them. And though they were taken captive to Babylon, there would be a time to leave.

Many who grew up there for seventy years had grown complacent and didn't want to go back to Jerusalem. Their children who were raised there never experienced the temple or the Promised Land and didn't want to go back. It is also said that many didn't want to leave Egypt either.

But now God said it was time to flee Babylon if they wanted to live, for it was the time of the Lord's vengeance. Babylon had been a golden cup in the Lord's hand that made all the earth drunk, which was why the nations foolishly boasted. Suddenly Babylon was fallen and destroyed as her judgment reached up to heaven.[40]

The Book of Revelation also says that all nations have drunk the wine of Babylon's sexual immorality and have grown rich from the power of her luxurious living. Then John heard another voice from heaven, paralleling what Jeremiah heard, that it was time to come out of Babylon lest you suffer the upcoming judgments because her sins have been heaped up till they reached heaven![41]

If you remember Daniel's prophecy of the different kingdoms making up the image of Nebuchadnezzar, you will remember that after Babylon came the Medes and the Persians. Jeremiah also informed his listeners that God was raising up the Medes to come against Babylon in vengeance for Babylon destroying His temple.[42] Jeremiah said that when God utters His voice, there is a multitude of waters in the heavens.[43] This reminds me of the verse in Revelation in which John also stated the voice that spoke to him had a voice like the sound of many waters.[44]

While the nations rely on idols that have no breath within them, the God of Israel controls all of nature. God proclaimed that Israel would be His battle-ax and weapon of war. With Israel

He would break in pieces the nations and destroy kingdoms. God would also render to Babylon all of the evil they did to Zion.[45]

The Bible then says that the sea would come upon Babylon and she would be covered by a multitude of waves.[46] I find it interesting that Babylon is surrounded by seas, but most are around six hundred miles away—the Mediterranean Sea to the west, the Black Sea and Caspian Sea to the north, and the Red Sea and Persian Gulf to the south. The Persian Gulf is the closest at a distance of around three hundred miles. There will have to be quite a flood if this is to take place literally.

God again called for His people to leave Babylon so as to not suffer His wrath when He poured it out.[47] As we close this chapter, we see that Jeremiah commanded that his next letter to Babylon would be by the hand of Seraiah, the son of Neriah, who was accompanied by King Zedekiah himself in the fourth year of his reign. Jeremiah put together all the evils that were coming to Babylon in a book, then gave it to Seraiah, telling him to read all the words and then let Babylon know that he had spoken against this place and it would be a ruin forever. When he had made an end of reading the book, he was to run for his life! Just kidding. When he was done, he was to tie a stone to it and throw it into the middle of the Euphrates, declaring that in this same way Babylon would sink and not rise from the evil that was coming.[48]

The fascinating connection with the Book of Revelation continues, where it is said concerning Babylon that a mighty angel took up a stone, like a great millstone, and cast it in to the sea, saying that with violence would the great city of Babylon be thrown down.[49]

People ask me who Babylon represents in these passages. The answer is multifaceted. Babylon can represent a political system, a religious system, literal Babylon, another nation, or a city. I have heard many examples, and as far as I am concerned, they can all be right at the same time! In Christianity we always look at things from a Western, Greek mindset, which is not how the Bible should be read. We believe there can only be one right answer, but that is not true. There are layers of interpretation that need to be considered.

Let's summarize some thoughts.

We need to acknowledge the pattern that God will always warn a people/nation before He brings judgment. We also see, though, that it is possible to do the work of the Lord deceitfully, bringing a curse upon the one who does. We also see that just as God judged the nations who mistreated Israel, once again that will happen.

Many of you know the parable in which God separates the sheep from the goats. He was not speaking of individuals but of nations. The nations who mistreated Israel will be punished severely. God's children are warned to flee Babylon, and I believe that speaks of a system that is alive and well today. It can be a political or a religious system, and often entails both. It is time for believers to cut themselves free from the love of this world.

QUESTIONS

- What is the Lord telling you about Himself?

- What else has the Lord taught you?

CHAPTER 14

UNDER THE YOKE

JEREMIAH 27–28, 21, 20, 37, AND 34

S O, IT WAS the fourth year of the reign of Zedekiah. It so happens it was also in the fifth month, the month of Av, which is around our July and August. Jeremiah was in the house of the Lord.[1] Let's return now to Jeremiah chapter 27.

It was time for Jeremiah to fulfill the prophecy that was spoken. After proclaiming all the woes to the various nations, the Lord told Jeremiah to make bonds and yokes, put them on his neck, and then send them by messengers to the kings of the Edomites, Moabites, and Ammonites, as well as the kings of Tyre and Zidon. God told Jeremiah to command them to tell their masters that the God of Israel, the One who made the earth as well as man and beast, was the One telling them that He was giving everything into the hand of Nebuchadnezzar, king of Babylon.[2]

Then He warned them that the nation that did not put their neck under the yoke of Babylon would be punished with the sword, famine, and pestilence until they were consumed. Therefore they were not to listen to false prophets, dreamers, enchanters, or sorcerers who told them not to serve Babylon. Those who obeyed this warning would be able to remain in their land, but those who didn't would be removed.[3]

Jeremiah then told King Zedekiah that he too must put his neck under the yoke of the king of Babylon. Why should he also die along with the people, by the sword, famine, and pestilence? He told Zedekiah not to listen to the prophets of Israel who were prophesying lies, using the Lord's name, and saying that the vessels taken from the Lord's house would be brought back shortly.[4] As a matter of fact every other vessel that remained in the house of the Lord would be taken to Babylon as well and would remain there until God brought them back in His time.[5]

Well, believe it or not, a false prophet named Hananiah came to Jeremiah and prophesied lies in the name of the Lord. Hananiah prophesied in the presence of all the other priests and all the people, claiming that the Lord said He had broken the yoke of the king of Babylon and that within two full years God would bring back all the vessels of the Lord's house that were taken to Babylon, along with King Jeconiah (Jehoiachin) and all the captives that were taken.[6]

Jeremiah didn't know whether this prophet heard from the Lord and was humble enough to admit he might be wrong, so Jeremiah said amen to that in the presence of all the priests and all the people.[7] As far as Jeremiah was concerned, that would be great news. Then Jeremiah warned everyone that a prophet who prophesies peace will be known as a true prophet when peace happens.[8] Hananiah took the yoke off Jeremiah's neck and broke it. He then spoke in the name of the Lord that God would break the yoke of Nebuchadnezzar, king of Babylon, from the neck of all nations within two years, and Jeremiah went on his merry way.[9]

Then, suddenly, the word of the Lord came to Jeremiah after Hananiah had broken the yoke off his neck. The Lord told Jeremiah to tell Hananiah that he might have broken yokes of wood, but now yokes of iron would be on the neck of all the nations. Then Jeremiah told him that because the Lord had not sent him and he made the people to trust in a lie, he would now be driven from the face of the earth! Remember this was in the fifth month. Now look at the rest of the prophecy Jeremiah gave him. He told Hananiah that he would die that year because he taught rebellion against the Lord. Then we find that he died two months later, in the seventh month.[10]

The seventh month is when Rosh Hashanah begins and then comes Yom Kippur ten days later. These are known as the ten days of awe and the day of judgment! Hananiah literally died during these days of awe. In the Book of Revelation we hear that the assembly in Smyrna will have tribulation for ten days.[11] This refers to the time frame of the ten days from Rosh Hashanah to Yom Kippur, which are known as the days of awe and the days of judgment, when the court of heaven is in session.

King Zedekiah then sent a couple of guys to Jeremiah by the names of Pashur and Zephaniah (not the prophet) to inquire what the word of the Lord was, as Nebuchadnezzar was now preparing for war, hoping perhaps the Lord would deal with them according to all His wonderful works and King Nebuchadnezzar would go away.[12] Definitely sounds as if they were trying to flatter Jeremiah. So Jeremiah told them to tell King Zedekiah that the weapons of war in his hands would be turned back as he was besieged by Nebuchadnezzar. They were then informed that God would help their enemy and assemble the Babylonians to fight them, and God Himself would join the fight against them with anger, fury, and great wrath. He would strike the inhabitants with great wrath, and they would all perish. Then God would take Zedekiah with all the people who survived the sword, famine, and pestilence into the hand of their enemies.[13] I wonder how they received those pleasantries from the mouth of Jeremiah!

Jeremiah was then told to give them a choice of life or death. He told them that whoever remained in Jerusalem would die, but whoever went outside and surrendered to the enemy would live. Jeremiah then told King Zedekiah that he better start executing judgment in the morning and deliver those who were being plundered by the oppressor.[14]

So now Pashur, the son of a priest who was also the chief governor in the house of the Lord, didn't like what Jeremiah was prophesying. He struck Jeremiah and put him in stocks in the high gate of Benjamin by the house of the Lord. The following day he removed Jeremiah, who told him that the Lord had not called his name Pashur, but Magormissabib (meaning fear on every side)! Then Jeremiah told Pashur that the Lord said he would even be a terror to himself and that all his friends would fall by the sword of their enemies and he would see it happen.[15]

The Lord went on to say that He would deliver all the wealth of the city, along with all its precious things, to their enemies, who would plunder them, seize them, and carry them off to Babylon. Oh, and by the way, God told Pashur that he and his whole family were going into captivity into Babylon, where he would die along with all his friends because he had prophesied lies.[16]

JEREMIAH IS MOCKED AND IMPRISONED

After Jeremiah's experience of being put in the stocks and slapped around, he had almost had enough. He declared that every day he was in derision because everyone mocked him. He would cry out, "Violence and spoil!" This was because the word of the Lord was made to him as a reproach every day. He decided he wouldn't mention the Lord's name or speak in His name anymore. He had one big problem though: he said that God's word in his heart was like a burning fire shut up in his bones. He was weary of trying to hold it back and just couldn't any longer.[17]

Jeremiah heard many people mocking him, saying, *"Fear on every side."* All of his acquaintances were watching for him to stumble, hoping they could prevail against him and take their revenge upon him.[18] Then Jeremiah realized that the Lord, who is mighty, was with him. Therefore all his persecutors were the ones who would stumble and be greatly ashamed.[19] Jeremiah was glad the poor were delivered from the evildoers but turned around and cursed the very day he was born. He said not to allow the day he was born to be blessed. He cursed the man who told his father he had a son, making him very glad. As a matter of fact Jeremiah said that man should be overthrown like the cities the Lord overthrew because Jeremiah wasn't slain from the womb, having his mother be his grave. He wondered why he was even born if all he was going to see was labor and sorrow and shame.[20]

Zedekiah decided to replace Pashur, so he sent Zephaniah back to Jeremiah with a man named Jehucal and asked Jeremiah to pray for them. Jeremiah had not yet been put in prison, and Pharaoh was coming from Egypt to help Jerusalem when he heard that it was being besieged by Babylon. The army of the Chaldeans was broken up from Jerusalem for fear of Pharaoh's army.[21] Then the word of the Lord came to Jeremiah to tell King Zedekiah, when he inquired of Jeremiah what the word of the Lord was, that Pharaoh's army that came to help you was returning to Egypt, the Babylonians were coming back, and they were going to burn the place down. Don't deceive yourself—the place would be burned down.[22]

So after the Chaldeans left Jerusalem for fear of Pharaoh's army, Jeremiah decided it was time to book it out of Jerusalem and head home to Anathoth in the land of Benjamin. That way at least he would be spared by not being in the city when the Babylonians returned. When he arrived at the Benjamin gate, a captain of the ward took him aside and asked him why he was surrendering to the Babylonians. Jeremiah said there was no way he would surrender; he just wanted to go home. But the captain didn't believe him and instead took him to the princes. The princes got all upset, smote him, and then put him in prison in the house of Jonathan the scribe. When Jeremiah had been in the dungeon many days, he was retrieved by Zedekiah and taken to his house. There Zedekiah asked Jeremiah secretly if there was a word from the Lord. Jeremiah informed him that there was and that he would be delivered into the hands of the king of Babylon.[23]

Then Jeremiah asked Zedekiah how he had offended the king, his servants, or the people that warranted his having to be put in prison. Jeremiah pleaded that he didn't want to go back to the house of Jonathan the scribe, where the prison was, because he knew he would die there. So King Zedekiah determined that he should be committed to the court of the prison and instead he should be a given daily a portion of bread from the baker. Fortunately for Jeremiah, he was allowed to remain in the court of the prison.[24]

We now go over to Ezekiel 1:1–3, and we find that on the fifth day of the fourth month in the thirtieth year, Ezekiel was sitting among the captives by the river Chebar. Suddenly the heavens were opened, and he saw visions of God. It was also the fifth year of King Jehoiachin's captivity. It was also the thirteenth year of Nebuchadnezzar.

How in the world do you make sense of all that? It's the thirtieth year of what? The fourth month is the month of Tammuz, which historically is the month that they had worshipped the golden calf. The fifth year of the captivity puts the date at 593 BC. The question is, When Ezekiel said it was the thirtieth year, what had happened thirty years earlier?

A couple of very important events happened! Thirty years earlier the scroll of the Torah was found and delivered to King Josiah. It just so happened it was also the thirtieth year of the Jubilee cycle. This was a very significant time! The Book of Ezekiel begins with his receiving a vision from God in an unclean land, but at least he was by a river, a somewhat clean place. He saw the likeness of the glory of the Lord, fell on his face, and heard the voice of One speaking.[25]

ZEDEKIAH—11 YEARS

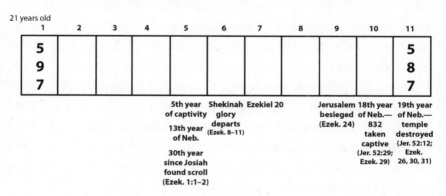

The voice spoke to Ezekiel, calling him "son of man." The Hebrew word for *man* here is *adam*. So there is a play on words, as Ezekiel was being called a son of Adam, not just a son of man. This is the first time ever in the Bible that the phrase *son of man* is used as a title. We also see that the spirit entered into Ezekiel when he was spoken to, and he was set on his feet.[26] I imagine that when the Spirit of God was breathed into Adam, he also was set on his feet.

Again the voice called him son of man/Adam, telling him to go to the rebellious nation of Israel that they might know a prophet was sent to them.[27] Just as Adam was given a command to not eat the fruit of the tree of the knowledge of good and evil but only eat of the tree of life, so now Ezekiel was given a command. Ezekiel was told to open his mouth and eat a scroll written within and without with lamentations, mourning, and woe.[28] He was to eat the scroll and then go and speak to the house of Israel. So he opened his mouth and ate the scroll, and it was as sweet as honey in his mouth.[29] I can't help but be reminded of when the apostle John was also told to eat a scroll, and in his mouth it was also as sweet as honey.[30] The Book of Revelation is definitely filled with lamentations, mourning, and woes.

From the Book of Ezekiel we find that in the following year, which was the sixth year of the captivity, on the fifth day of the sixth month, the elders were sitting before Ezekiel in Babylon, and the hand of the Lord came upon Ezekiel.[31] The sixth month is the month of Elul, which is in our August to September time frame. It is known as the month of repentance, as it is the month before the fall feasts of Rosh Hashanah, Yom Kippur, and Sukkot. Elul is also the month Moses ascended Mount Sinai the second time for forty days to make atonement for the sin of the golden calf, and it is also the same time that Yeshua went into the wilderness for forty days in preparation for His ministry.

This hand of the Lord in Ezekiel is described as having the appearance of fire. This hand grabbed Ezekiel by a lock of his hair, and the Spirit lifted him into the atmosphere between earth and heaven and brought him to Jerusalem, where he saw the glory of the God of Israel.[32] Can you imagine being grabbed by a lock of your hair and then being suspended a mile into the air, swinging in the wind?

Ezekiel saw at the entrance to the northern gate an altar called an "image of jealousy." Ezekiel was then brought to the door of the court, and he saw a hole in the wall and then a door. He went through the door and saw all kinds of abominable things. There were idols portrayed on the walls and seventy men with censers that had a thick cloud of incense ascending up. These men felt the Lord could not see what they were doing. God then brought Ezekiel to the northern gate of the Lord's house, and there he saw women sitting and weeping for Tammuz. The Lord took Ezekiel farther in, and he saw twenty-five men with their backs toward the temple and their faces toward the east, worshipping the sun.[33]

All of this was happening during the second half of Zedekiah's reign. It was in the sixth year of Zedekiah that the shekinah glory abandoned the temple. Read all about it in Ezekiel chapters 8–11.

God had had enough! The glory left five years before the temple was destroyed. A voice cried out that those who had charge over the city were to draw near with their destroying weapons in their hand. Six men went to the higher gate, and one of these men was clothed in linen with a writer's inkhorn by his side. They went in and stood by the brazen altar. The glory of the God of Israel had gone up from the cherub, and the Lord told the man with the inkhorn to go through the midst of the city and set a mark upon the foreheads of the men who were crying because of all the abominations that were going on in the city.[34]

The Hebrew word for *mark* is not only a word but a Hebrew letter. It is the last letter of the Hebrew alphabet, the letter *tav*. In English we get our letter *t* from this Hebrew letter. In the ancient Hebrew the letter actually looked like our small letter *t*, being in the form of a cross. It also was turned to the right much like in the form of our letter x. The Hebrew word *tav* means a mark or a signature. Using the letter x for a signature comes from this ancient Hebrew concept. It was their mark. So all the righteous Jews had this mark put on their foreheads so they would be spared!

We find that the glory of the Lord then went up from the cherub and stood over the threshold of the house as the house was filled with the cloud and the court was full of the Lord's glory.[35] The glory then departed from the threshold and stood over the cherubim. The cherubim lifted their wings and mounted up from the earth in the sight of Ezekiel while everyone stood at the door of the east gate of the Lord's house, having the glory of the God of Israel over them.[36]

The Spirit then lifted Ezekiel and brought him to the eastern gate of the Lord's house. God showed Ezekiel twenty-five of the most wicked men in the city giving bad counsel. Ezekiel prophesied, and one of them fell down dead.[37] Then the cherubim lifted up their wings, and the glory of the Lord went up from the midst of the city and stood on the Mount of Olives.[38] I find it interesting that the glory left from the Mount of Olives; that is also where Yeshua ascended and where the glory will return![39]

In the seventh year of Zedekiah, on the tenth day of the fifth month, some of the elders of Israel came to Ezekiel to inquire of the Lord.[40] This is the month of Av, which again is around July/August. The ninth day of the month of Av was a cursed date, as that was the date the ten spies had brought the bad report in the time of Moses and would also be the very date the temple would be destroyed twice, in 587/586 BC and then again in AD 70.

Back in Jerusalem, we see the word of the Lord now came to Jeremiah when Nebuchadnezzar had Jerusalem surrounded and was fighting against it. Jeremiah went to speak to King Zedekiah. He was to tell him that the city was done for and would be burned with fire.[41] Great news to be giving the king!

So what's new? you may ask. Well, you will see that God's mercy extends to the uttermost. One of the reasons God is determined to do evil upon a city is when the rulers continually heap all their transgressions one upon another. Do you remember after 9/11 when many people turned to God for a short while before it was back to same old same old? It comes across as a false repentance.

Well, such was the case with Zedekiah. He had decided to obey at least one commandment as if God would be impressed. Which commandment did he think might stop the hand of judgment coming upon him? There was a commandment that at the end of seven years a release was to be made of servants, and debts were to be cancelled. They were to proclaim liberty to all servants by setting them free.[42]

Also, at the end of every seventh year, in the solemnity of the year of release, when all of Israel was to come and appear before the Lord in Jerusalem, the Law was to be read to every man, woman, and child so that they might hear and do the word of the Lord.[43] So, here we are, in the seventh year, known also as the sabbatical year or the shemitah year, and what do we find out happened?

Zedekiah wanted to curry God's favor and made a covenant with all the people in Jerusalem to proclaim liberty to them. He said that every man should allow their Hebrew manservants and maidservants to go free. We find that all the princes and all the people heard they should release their servants, so they entered the covenant, obeyed, and let their servants go. But then they turned after they let them go free, and they caused all their servants and handmaids to return whom they had set free and brought them back into subjection![44]

Why do you think this happened? I'll tell you why. It was a shemitah year, and with Babylon coming, they were in total fear, so they cried out to God and read from the Torah. When Egypt came to their aid, causing the Babylonians to retreat, they figured the Egyptians were the ones who chased off the Babylonians, therefore Egypt should get all the credit, and it wasn't God who helped them at all! Or maybe when that disaster had been averted, they still really needed the servants, so they decided to ditch the agreement.

So the word of the Lord came to Jeremiah, and the Lord declared that He had made a covenant with their fathers when they left Egypt out of the house of slaves, telling them that after six years they were to let their servants go in the seventh year. He said their fathers never listened to Him, and now they did what was right in proclaiming liberty and entering into a covenant before Him, in the house called by His name, but they had polluted it. Therefore God said He would proclaim liberty to them. They were going to get a special liberty—one to the sword, to pestilence, to famine, and they would be removed into all the kingdoms of the earth.[45] The Lord was now commanding Babylon to come back to the city, fight against it, and burn it down till there were no inhabitants.[46]

Let's summarize some thoughts.

God is the One who raises up and puts down nations. Think of the nations that have persecuted the Jewish people throughout history. Where are they now?

It is important to realize that if you enter into a covenant with God, you better follow through with it. So often people cry out to God when they are in trouble, declaring all kinds of vows, and then don't follow through. There will be accountability!

QUESTIONS

- What is the Lord telling you about Himself?

- What else has the Lord taught you?

CHAPTER 15

IN THE PRISON

JEREMIAH 33, 38, AND 32

Now, THE WORD of the Lord came a second time to Jeremiah while he was shut up in the court of the prison, telling him to call on the Lord and He would show him great and mighty things that he didn't know.[1] If it were me, I'd be asking something such as "When in the world are You ever going to get me out of here?"

God then not only pronounced judgment, but He also let Jeremiah know the good news that He would cause the captivity of both the house of Israel and the house of Judah to return, and He would rebuild them, cleanse them from all their iniquity, and pardon all their transgressions.[2] Jerusalem would become a name of joy, a praise, and an honor before all the nations of the earth when they heard of all the good that God did for them. There was even a promise that while the streets of Jerusalem had become a desolation without man or beast, the voice of joy and the voice of gladness, along with the voice of the bridegroom and the voice of the bride, would be heard again—and even the voice of those who said, "The Lord is good, For His mercy endures forever."[3]

God reemphasized to Jeremiah that in spite of all the desolations, there would be habitations of shepherds causing their flocks to lie down. There was still a hope for a future day when God would perform all the good that He had promised. The Lord would cause the Branch of righteousness to grow up to David, and He would be the One to execute both judgment and righteousness in the land.[4]

We now find that Jerusalem would finally dwell safely, and it had a new name as well. Jerusalem would be called "The Lord our righteousness," or Jehovah Tzidkenu. David would never lack a man to sit on the throne of the house of Israel, and neither would a priest from the Levites ever lack a man to offer burnt offerings to sacrifice continually.[5]

This is a huge prophecy. Don't miss everything it is telling us. It says the sacrificial system will be reinstituted, along with the Levitical priesthood. This means the Catholic priesthood will be history. Sacrifices will be restored.

Perhaps, like many, you can understand Yeshua sitting on the throne of David but can't wrap your head around the continual sacrificial system being restored. Rather than accepting the obvious, many people try to rationalize the sacrificial system away theologically. I feel it is better to consider that maybe Christians have never really understood the sacrificial system due to their abandonment of the Hebraic mindset, and rather than tossing it out, we should take an honest look at what God says in Ezekiel and discover what God has always wanted us to learn from it.

There will be sacrifices again when the temple is rebuilt by the Messiah for the thousand-year reign. He will even be there Himself to accept the offerings. We find this confirmed in the Book of Jeremiah, in which the Lord said that if anyone could break His covenant of day and night so that day and night ceased, only then could His covenant to David be broken so that he wouldn't have a son to reign on his throne. He also said that the covenant He had with Levites would not end. Just as the stars of heaven cannot be numbered or the sand of the sea, God said He would multiply the seed of David and the Levites who minister to Him.[6]

The word of the Lord came again to Jeremiah, telling him to consider what the enemies of God were saying. God's adversaries were spreading fake news that the two families that the Lord chose, Israel and Judah, had been cast off. They despised and condemned God's people and said that Israel should no more be a nation before them. So the Lord reassured Jeremiah that He would no more reject His people than He would break His covenant with day and night, or heaven and earth. He promised to never abandon the descendants of Jacob or change His plan to have David's seed rule over the seed of Abraham, Isaac, and Jacob.[7]

While the Lord was speaking to Jeremiah, several princes got wind that Jeremiah had told all the people the Lord had said whoever remained in the city would die by the sword, famine, and pestilence, but whoever surrendered to the Babylonians would live. The princes were not happy about this. So they told the king to have Jeremiah put to death because he was weakening the hands of the men of war who remained in the city by saying such things. They believed Jeremiah was not seeking the welfare of everyone but only seeking their hurt. So Zedekiah the king told them that Jeremiah was now in their hands, for the king was not one who could do anything against them.[8]

This is mind-blowing to me. What a weak-kneed king. What a wimp. This reminds me of Israel's first king, Saul, who also said he feared the people and, therefore, did not obey God.[9] I fear God much more than I do people. What about you?

So they took Jeremiah and lowered him with cords into the dungeon in the court of the prison. It just so happened there was an Ethiopian servant in the king's house named Ebedmelech, who heard that they had put Jeremiah in the dungeon. He went and spoke to the king, telling him that there were people who had done evil to Jeremiah by casting him into the dungeon and he would certainly die of hunger as the city was now completely out of bread. So the king told Ebedmelech to grab thirty men and get Jeremiah out before he died. Ebedmelech got some old rags and lowered them to Jeremiah, who put them under his arms under the cords. So Jeremiah was lifted up out of the dungeon, but he still remained in the court of the prison.[10]

After that, King Zedekiah had Jeremiah brought to the house of the Lord and again sought to ask Jeremiah a question, wanting Jeremiah to hide nothing from him. Nothing but the truth! Jeremiah asked him why in the world he would tell him the truth, when the king was only going to kill him for it! Not only that, the king wouldn't do what Jeremiah said anyway.

So the king swore that he wouldn't put Jeremiah to death or hand him over to those who wanted to kill him. Jeremiah spoke the word of the Lord to the king, telling him that if he would just surrender, not only would he live but so would his family, and the city would not be burned by fire. But if he didn't, the city would be burned to the ground and he would not escape.[11]

The king confessed to Jeremiah that he was afraid of the Jews who had already surrendered to the Babylonians and that he would be delivered into their hands and then be mocked by them.[12] Talk about a total narcissist! He was willing to have the entire city burned to the ground and his family killed just so he wouldn't be mocked. Unbelievable. We do have to remember, though, that the king was only around thirty-one years old at this time too.

Jeremiah assured the king that what he feared wouldn't happen and implored him again to obey the voice of the Lord so it would be well with him. He also reiterated that if the king refused, it would be all over and the city would be burned with fire. Then King Zedekiah told Jeremiah to keep their conversation a secret and then Jeremiah wouldn't die. But if the princes came to Jeremiah to ask him what was said, Jeremiah was to tell them that he asked the king not to send him back to Jonathan the scribe's house to die. Well, it just so happened that the princes did ask Jeremiah that very thing. Jeremiah told them exactly what the king had said to tell them. Therefore they left him, and Jeremiah remained in the court of the prison until the day that Jerusalem was taken.[13]

A Day Israel Would Never Forget

We now find out that in Zedekiah's ninth year Nebuchadnezzar returned, and on the tenth day of the tenth month, Nebuchadnezzar besieged Jerusalem with his entire army, building forts all around it, until the eleventh and final year of King Zedekiah.[14]

This was a day that would forever live in biblical history and a day the Lord would never forget. God even spoke to Ezekiel, who was being held captive in Babylon, to make a record of this day.

The Lord came to Ezekiel in the ninth year, on the tenth day of the tenth month, telling him to write the name of that very day that the king of Babylon set himself against Jerusalem. The

Lord told Ezekiel to utter a parable to the rebellious house, and He told him to start cooking! He was to get a pot, pour water in it, fill it with some good soup bones, put in some choice portions from the flock, and then let it simmer. The Lord declared a woe to the bloody city, to the pot that was filled with scum.[15]

This day is known as the tenth day of the month of Tevet, which is usually around late December and early January. This day has become a major fast day every year for the last 2,500 years. We find this from the Book of Zechariah, in which the Lord prophesied that the fasts of the fourth month, the fifth month, the seventh month, and the tenth month would become to the house of Judah joy and gladness and cheerful feasts.[16]

Each one of these fasts has to do with the destruction of Jerusalem during the time of Jeremiah. We have just learned that the fast of the tenth month is connected to when Jerusalem was besieged for the final time. The fast of the fourth month is the seventeenth of Tammuz, when the walls of Jerusalem were broken down, giving Nebuchadnezzar access. And the fast of the fifth month is the ninth of Av, when the temple was destroyed. Lastly the fast of the seventh month is in recognition of when the man who was put in charge of Jerusalem by Nebuchadnezzar, Gedaliah, was murdered.

If we as Christians aren't on the biblical calendar and know nothing of these events or the dates when they happened on our calendar, how will we ever know when this prophecy from 2,500 years ago is fulfilled? This is why my ministry produces a biblical calendar that you can get from us at www.elshaddaiministries.us so you will be aware of God's calendar and see the significant dates when these things happened!

A year had gone by, and the word of the Lord came to Jeremiah in the tenth year of Zedekiah, king of Judah, which was also the eighteenth year of Nebuchadnezzar. Babylon was besieging

Jerusalem, and Jeremiah was shut up in the court of the prison, all because of his words declaring that Jerusalem would be given over to the hands of Nebuchadnezzar.[17]

Can you feel the tension of the times? Imagine how Jeremiah felt being locked up in the midst of a war going on just outside the walls, with nowhere to run.

What happens to real estate values in a city being bombed or invaded by another country that plans to either burn the houses to the ground or take over the houses and kill the inhabitants so they can move into their homes? At that very moment in history, God told Jeremiah that his uncle's son, Hanameel, was coming to ask him if he would please buy his field in Anathoth, where Jeremiah was from, because Jeremiah had the right of redemption to buy it. When this happened, Jeremiah definitely knew he just heard from God![18]

He bought the property, and when the evidence of the purchase was delivered to Baruch, Jeremiah prayed to the Lord, declaring that there was nothing too difficult for the God who made heaven and earth by His great power and outstretched arm![19]

I hope Jeremiah got a good price. But one thing is for sure: Jeremiah trusted the Lord that Israel would be brought back to life.

The Lord brought Israel out of Egypt with all kinds of signs and wonders, with a strong hand, and with an outstretched arm. He gave them the Promised Land that He swore to give to their fathers, a land flowing with milk and honey, and they even came in and possessed it. But they would not obey God's voice or walk in His Law, doing nothing of all that He commanded them, which is why all this evil befell them.[20]

God told Jeremiah His anger was provoked by all of the evil the children of Israel and the children of Judah had done, as well as all the inhabitants of Jerusalem. They had turned their backs to God and not their faces. Even though God taught them, they would not receive instruction.[21]

I find it interesting that the Hebrew word translated into English as "receive instruction" could also be translated that they would not "accept morality." Instead they set up their abominations in the house called by God's name to defile it. They built high places of Baal in the Valley of the Son of Hinnom to cause their sons and daughters to pass through the fire to Molech, which God never commanded nor did it even enter His mind to do such an abominable thing.[22]

We know, though, that God is a covenant-keeping God, so we find that the Lord said He would still gather them out of all the countries that He had scattered them to, bring them back to the Promised Land, and cause them to dwell safely. They would be His people, and He would be their God. He was going to give them one heart so that they would fear Him forever. He would make an everlasting covenant with them to do them good. He would put His fear in their hearts so they wouldn't depart from Him. He would also rejoice over them and replant them in the land with His whole heart and soul. The Lord keeps His promises. He had brought all the evil that was promised, and now He promised that He would also bring all the good.[23]

When we see what was happening at this time in Babylon, we read that Ezekiel was also hearing from the Lord. In the tenth year, on the twelfth day of the tenth month, the word of the Lord came to Ezekiel, telling him to set his face against Pharaoh and prophesy against him, letting him know that God was against him. He compared Pharaoh to the great dragon lying in the midst of the rivers, claiming that the river belonged to him and he was the one who created it.[24]

Then in the eleventh year of Zedekiah, on the seventh day of the first month, the word of the Lord came again to Ezekiel, telling him that the Lord had broken the arms of Pharaoh so that his sword would fall from his hands.[25] The first month is the month of Nisan, when Passover is observed, around our March and April. We are told that it was in the eleventh and final year of Zedekiah, on the first day of the third month, that the word of the Lord came again to Ezekiel, basically telling him to tell Pharaoh he was full of pride.[26]

The third month is the month of Sivan, which is when the Feast of Shavuot, or Pentecost, is observed. The Jews have been celebrating this feast for the last 3,500 years. I also want to point out to you that prophecies from the Lord are always based on timing. The prophecies come on the appointed times of the new moons, as on the first day of a month, or around one of the feast days.

All of these prophetic messages went to Egypt because that's where the remnant of Jews were heading after kidnapping Jeremiah and taking him along with them. Nebuchadnezzar was the one coming to judge Egypt. The following year, in the twelfth year of captivity, it was around 586 BC and we find on the first day of the twelfth month, the word of the Lord came to Ezekiel. God told him to take up a lamentation for Pharaoh, telling him he was done for.[27]

Not too long after the temple was destroyed, Ezekiel heard about its destruction. The temple was destroyed in the fifth month, and now on the fifth day of the tenth month, one of those who had escaped Jerusalem arrived and told him that the city had been smitten.[28] This was also the time when the word of the Lord came to Ezekiel to inform him that those with him in Babylon were being pretentious when they told him he sang beautifully, wrote wonderful songs, and played his instrument well. God said they didn't do a word He had said![29]

Let's summarize some thoughts.

We see that God keeps His word and His covenant. This is so important to realize. God has not replaced the covenant with Israel with a Gentile covenant. Also we see the importance again of the biblical calendar, as prophecies are almost always given according to the appointed times.

Questions

- What is the Lord telling you about Himself?

- What else has the Lord taught you?

CHAPTER 16

OFF TO EGYPT

JEREMIAH 39–43

L ET'S GO BACK a moment to the eleventh and final year of the reign of Zedekiah. It was the fourth month and the ninth day of the month. The fourth month is the month of Tammuz and would be around our June/July time frame. The city was broken up, and all the princes of Babylon were sitting in the middle gate of the city. King Zedekiah saw them with all the men of war, so he fled with others out of the city during the night by the way of the king's garden.[1]

But the Chaldeans chased after them and overtook Zedekiah in the plains of Jericho. They took him to meet Nebuchadnezzar in Riblah, where he forced Zedekiah to watch his sons being killed. He then put out Zedekiah's eyes, so that would be the last thing Zedekiah saw. Then they bound him with chains and carried him off to Babylon, putting him in prison until he died at age thirty-two.[2]

The Chaldeans burned down the king's house and all the other houses, and then they broke down the walls of Jerusalem. Nebuzaradan, the captain of the guard, took the remnant in the city, along with those who had surrendered, to Babylon. He did leave the poor people of the land who didn't have anything, giving them the vineyards and fields. Nebuchadnezzar ordered Nebuzaradan to do Jeremiah no harm, to look well to him, and to do whatever Jeremiah asked of him. So Nebuzaradan had the princes of Babylon take Jeremiah out of the court of the prison and committed him to Gedaliah, the son of Ahikam, the son of Shaphan, to carry him home![3]

This is huge! Do you realize just who Gedaliah was? Shaphan was the one with Hilkiah when the scroll of the Lord was found back in Josiah's day.[4] His son Ahikam was the one who protected Jeremiah.[5] Now we would see that this Gedaliah was the one Nebuchadnezzar now appointed over Jerusalem.

Jeremiah Is Released From Prison

As Jeremiah was freed, we find out that while he was still in the court of the prison, the nice Ethiopian guard Ebedmelech, who was concerned for his life, was told by Jeremiah, through the word of the Lord, that while the Lord was bringing His word to fruition in destroying the city, Ebedmelech would be delivered because He had put his trust in the Lord.[6]

Nebuzaradan then made a startling statement to Jeremiah. He told Jeremiah that the Lord his God had pronounced evil on the place and the Lord brought it just like He said because they had sinned against the Lord and had not obeyed His voice.[7] How would you feel if you were Jeremiah after hearing this?

Nebuzaradan then told Jeremiah that he could go wherever he wanted—to Babylon, where he would be well taken care of, or wherever he might want to go in the land. He then suggested to Jeremiah that he might want to go back to Gedaliah, whom the king made governor. He fed Jeremiah, gave him a reward, and then let him go. Jeremiah looked at his options and decided to head to Gedaliah, who was in Mizpah.[8]

When the captains of the forces of Israel in the fields heard that Gedaliah was made governor, those who were left in the land came to him. In particular there were two captains, Johanan and Ishmael. Gedaliah told them they were not to fear the Chaldeans, but just dwell in the land and all would be well if they would serve the king of Babylon.[9] The Jews who had fled to the other countries of Moab, Amon, and Edom also came to Gedaliah and gathered wine and all the summer fruits.[10]

Johanan told Gedaliah secretly that he wanted to be allowed to go and kill Ishmael because Ishmael wanted to secretly kill Gedaliah! Gedaliah thought Johanan was speaking falsely about Ishmael, so he told Johanan not to kill Ishmael.[11] In the seventh month, which is the month of Tishri, around our September/October and also when the fall feasts occur (notice the timing), Ishmael, who was of the royal line, came with ten men to Gedaliah. As they were eating together, Ishmael rose up with his ten men and slew Gedaliah with the sword and killed the other Jews and Chaldeans who were with him.[12]

Ishmael then carried away captive all who were left in Mizpah, even the king's daughters, who were put in Gedaliah's care. He headed for the Ammonite area, but when Johanan, along with his forces, heard what happened, they took all their men and went after him. They found him by the great waters of Gibeon. When the captives of Ishmael saw all the forces of Johanan, they were very glad and ran over to Johanan.[13]

Then the captains of the forces and all the remnant of the people who were left came to the prophet Jeremiah, begging him to pray for them to the Lord his God that the Lord his God might show them where to go and what to do.[14] I find it very fascinating that both times they didn't say the Lord our God but only the Lord his God.

Jeremiah told them that he heard them, he would pray to the Lord their God, and whatever the Lord told him, he would relate to them. Then they said to Jeremiah, in essence making a vow, that as the Lord was a true and faithful witness between them, they would do according to whatever the Lord said to Jeremiah; whether it was for good or for evil, they would obey the message from the Lord their God. They said this was so that it would go well with them when they did obey the voice of the Lord their God.[15] Twice they finally laid claim to the fact that the Lord was their God too. So Jeremiah sought the Lord for what He would say to this motley crew.

After ten days the word of the Lord came to Jeremiah, so he had everyone come together to hear what the Lord had said. Jeremiah told them the Lord God of Israel said that if they stayed in Israel, the Lord would build them and not pull them down, plant them and not pluck them up, because He repented of the evil He had done to them. Twice the Lord told them not to be afraid of the king of Babylon because the Lord would save them and deliver them from his hand. The Lord would even show mercies to them and cause them to return to the land.[16]

Then came the warning! Jeremiah warned them that if they decided to not dwell in the land of Israel, they did not want to obey the voice of the Lord their God, and they decided to go down to Egypt instead, then their fears would come upon them and the sword would overtake them. The famine would also follow them in Egypt, and there they would die. Everyone who set their faces to go to Egypt would die by the sword, famine, and pestilence, and none of them would escape the evil He would bring upon them. The Lord told them that just as His anger and fury was brought on the inhabitants of Jerusalem, it would then be poured out on them as well when they entered Egypt. There they would be considered an execration, an astonishment, a curse, and a reproach, and they would never be allowed back into Israel. Whatever they did, they had now been officially warned not to go back to Egypt.[17]

We have to remember that the whole group, along with the captains of the forces, vowed they would do whatever the Lord said for their good, no matter what. But now we find Jeremiah telling them they were hypocrites when they sent him to the Lord to pray for them and insisted that they would do whatever the Lord said. He therefore declared to them that they had not obeyed the voice of the Lord their God or anything else in which He had sent them to Jeremiah. Jeremiah told them they would certainly die by the sword, famine, and pestilence when they went to Egypt.[18]

When Jeremiah had finished relaying the word of the Lord to them, all the proud men, including Johanan, told Jeremiah he was lying. They said he was a false prophet and that the Lord never told him to tell them not go into Egypt to live. They said that Baruch, his scribe, was the one who turned Jeremiah against them that they might fall into the hands of the Chaldeans, who would kill them and carry them away as captives into Babylon. So Johanan, with all the captains of the forces as well as all the people, decided not to obey the voice of the Lord, that they should dwell in the land of Israel.[19]

We know the Lord is the same yesterday, today, and forever. Written in the Torah, almost a thousand years earlier, God told them that they were never to return to Egypt.[20] But Johanan and the captains of the forces took captive Jeremiah, Baruch, and all the remnant of Judah that had returned, as well as all those who had remained in the land being put in the care of Gedaliah, and hauled them off to Egypt![21]

So they came into Egypt in total disobedience to the Lord, landing in the city of Tahpanhes. Now the word of the Lord came to Jeremiah while he was in Egypt, telling him to take great stones into his hands and to hide them in the brick kiln at the entry of Pharaoh's house, in the sight of the men of Judah. Jeremiah was then to tell them that Nebuchadnezzar, the king of Babylon, was God's servant, and he would set his throne on these very stones Jeremiah had hidden at the entry of Pharaoh's house. When Nebuchadnezzar arrived, he would smite the land of Egypt, killing all those appointed to death and taking captive all those appointed to captivity. Then God would kindle a fire in the houses of all the gods of Egypt, and Nebuchadnezzar would burn the places down and take the people captive. Nebuchadnezzar would wear Egypt like a shepherd's cloak as he left there in complete triumph.[22]

Let's summarize some thoughts.

I find it amazing that the people swore that they would do whatever the Lord said for them to do, and then when they heard it, they insisted that Jeremiah heard wrong. How often do we say we will obey God at any cost, but in reality we are only willing to hear from people who tell us what we want to hear?

QUESTIONS

- What is the Lord telling you about Himself?

- What else has the Lord taught you?

CHAPTER 17

THERE IS NO KING

JEREMIAH 44 AND 52

W HEN JEREMIAH WAS in Egypt, the word of the Lord came
to him concerning all the Jews who were dwelling there
with him. They were now scattered into several cities, dwelling in
Migdol, Tahpanhes, Noph, and in the area of Pathros. The word
to the people was that they had seen all the evil that the God of
Israel did to His own land and His own city, Jerusalem, as well
as on all the other cities of Judah. They had become a desolation
where no one dwelled because of the wickedness they had committed in provoking Him to anger by their burning of incense to
other gods.[1]

Again, if they had only heeded the warnings written down
almost a thousand years earlier when God warned them that if
they did as the other nations did in their wickedness, the land

would vomit them out just like the others.[2] The word of the Lord is forever, and who is man to think he can edit God's Word, claiming this or that is done away with?

The Lord went on to say that in spite of their wickedness. Rising early, He had sent all of His servants, the prophets, telling them to warn the people not to do the abominable things He hated in His sight. They never listened or even tried to hear to turn from their wickedness in their burning incense to other gods. That is why God's fury and wrath was poured out, and the cities of Judah had been wasted. Therefore the Lord, the God of armies, asked them why they were committing this great evil against their own souls by provoking Him to wrath with the work of their hands by continuing to burn incense to other gods even while they were in Egypt where they were now living.[3]

Were they wanting to be totally cut off, becoming a curse among all the nations of the earth? Had they already forgotten the wickedness of their fathers, the wickedness of the kings of Judah, and the wickedness of their wives committed in the land of Israel? They had never humbled themselves, feared God, or walked in His laws or statutes that He had set before them or their fathers. The Lord said that He was now setting His face against them for evil.[4] Their response was unbelievable!

All the men who knew their wives had burned incense to the other gods, all the women standing by, and a great multitude of all those who were dwelling in Egypt basically told Jeremiah to stuff it! Whatever Jeremiah said the word of the Lord was, they weren't going to listen. They were going to do whatever came out of their own mouths, and they were going to continue to burn incense to the queen of heaven, pouring out drink offerings to her, just as their fathers, their kings, and their princes had done in all of the land of Israel. They believed burning incense to the queen of heaven had brought them prosperity where they had seen no evil, but it was really the fact that they had stopped burning incense to her. The women who had been burning incense, pouring drink offerings, and making cakes to worship to the queen of heaven asked Jeremiah if he really thought the men weren't involved as well.[5]

So Jeremiah responded to them, asking if they really thought the Lord didn't remember or it didn't come into His mind. The real problem was that the Lord could no longer bear all the evil of their doings, and that was why the land had become a desolation.[6]

Not only that, by the word of the Lord Jeremiah told all those living in Egypt that as they had spoken, declaring they would fulfill their vows to burn incense and pour out drink offerings to the queen of heaven, therefore they would perform their vows. So then Jeremiah reported that the Lord swore by His great name that His name would no more be named in any of the mouths of the men of Judah who were in Egypt. The Lord would now watch over them for evil and not for good. Yet a small number would yet escape Egypt and return to the land of Israel. The Lord then gave them a sign that they would know His words were against them. God was going to give Pharaohhophra, king of Egypt, into the hands of his enemies just as he did to King Zedekiah.[7]

THE PROPHET EZEKIEL

We find in the twenty-fifth year of the captivity, in the beginning of the year, on the tenth day of the month, in the fourteenth year after the city was smitten, the hand of the Lord came on Ezekiel.[8] This would be 573 BC on Yom Kippur in a Jubilee year! We see God gave Ezekiel a vision and set Ezekiel high on a very high mountain in the land of Israel. He beheld a man whose appearance was like brass, holding a line of flax and a measuring reed in his hand.[9]

Ezekiel began to measure all the gates. Afterward Ezekiel was brought to the gate that faced east, and he beheld the glory of the God of Israel coming from that direction; His voice was like the noise of many waters, and the earth shined with His glory.[10] We also see these future gates of the temple would all be named after the twelve tribes of Israel.[11]

These verses remind me of the Book of Revelation, in which another angel had a reed and was measuring Jerusalem. John was also carried away to a very high mountain and saw the great city, holy Jerusalem.[12]

Then we see in the Book of Jeremiah that in the thirty-seventh year of Jehoiachin's captivity, on the twenty-fifth day of the twelfth month, Evilmerodach, the king of Babylon, in the first year of his reign, decided to free Jehoiachin, bringing him out of prison. He spoke kindly to him, exalted him upon a throne, putting him over the other kings that were with him in Babylon. He gave him a change of garments and allowed him to sit at the king's table and enjoy all he could eat for the rest of his life.[13] The twelfth month is the month of Adar, equivalent to our February/March. The thirty-seventh year of Jehoiachin's captivity would have been 560 BC.

Let's summarize some thoughts.

Even after experiencing all of God's judgments in Israel and being exiled to Egypt, God's people continued to disobey. This was for us to realize that it was the goodness of God that leads men to true repentance. God's wrath was not for the purpose of bringing repentance but judgment. Preaching hellfire and brimstone only hardens the hearts of most people, as it did to Pharaoh.

God sets before us blessing and cursing to motivate us to choose correctly. While He punishes us as a form of correction to stop us in our tracks so we repent, when His wrath is poured out, it is not to lead to repentance anymore. When He pours out His wrath, His servants are sealed.

QUESTIONS

- What is the Lord telling you about Himself?

- What else has the Lord taught you?

CHAPTER 18

LAMENTATIONS

AMENTATIONS IS REALLY quite the book. Jeremiah was lamenting the destruction of the temple and Jerusalem, as well as the people being scattered. I find this book fascinating. It reminds me of the game Jenga, where the blocks are all stacked upon each other in different directions. When the wrong block is pulled out, the whole thing falls apart, tumbling to the ground.

Lamentations has five chapters. Most people are not aware, but the book is written as an acrostic that you can only recognize in the Hebrew language. There are twenty-two letters in the Hebrew alphabet, and there are twenty-two verses in chapter one. Each verse starts with a successive letter of the Hebrew alphabet.

For example, in English the first verse would begin with a word that starts with the letter *a*. The second verse would have the letter *b* as the first letter of the first word, continuing on until the twenty-sixth verse began with a *z* word. Because the acrostic follows the Hebrew alphabet, in English translations we would never see the order.

But an enigma takes place in the second chapter. There are still twenty-two verses patterned after the Hebrew alphabet, but this time two letters are reversed in their order. The letter *ayin* now comes right before the letter *pe*.

Since we know God has a reason and a purpose for everything that He does and says, what is the meaning of this anomaly? In Hebrew every letter is also a word. The letter *ayin* is the word meaning to see, know, or understand. The letter *pe* refers to the mouth or to speech. The idea is that we should understand a topic before we speak about it. So the first chapter is in alphabetical order, and the second chapter is almost in complete order, but two letters are reversed, as the *pe* now comes before the *ayin*. This is telling us that they are now speaking before they know what they are talking about.

Interestingly enough it is also said that what destroyed the temple was *sinat chinam*, which is known as baseless hatred. The people would speak only falsehoods. I can't help but notice all the baseless hatred that is in our world today, along with all of the evil speech and fake news going around.

This brings us to the third chapter of Lamentations. The third chapter has sixty-six verses, and the reason is that this time there are three verses in a row given to each letter. So the first three verses all begin with words that start with the letter *aleph*. The *pe* and the *ayin* are still in reversed order.

The fourth chapter is then back to the twenty-two verses in alphabetical order, except the *ayin* and the *pe* are still in reverse order. The fifth and final chapter again has twenty-two verses, but this time the letters are all scrambled with no rhyme or reason, just as it appears in the English. To me this shows that everything has descended into complete chaos. Let's take a look now at this heartbreaking message from Jeremiah in the Book of Lamentations.

CHAPTER 1: HOW?

The first word in the first verse is interesting. In English the word is *how*. Jeremiah is wondering how in the world all of this happened. The city that was full of inhabitants was now empty.[1] In this book there are no "words from the Lord" for Jeremiah; it is mostly just a cry from the depths of his heart about how has all this happened.

Jerusalem had gone from being the beauty of all the earth to the despised of all the earth. She had gone from receiving tributary to becoming tributary.[2] According to the word of the Lord to Ezekiel, her renown went forth among the nations because of her beauty, but she ended up trusting in her own beauty and playing the harlot because of her renown. She took all of what the Lord had given to her and gave it to her idols.[3]

As believers, when we see big names or ministries fall by the wayside, we also often wonder how in the world it happened. History always repeats itself over and over, and as I've already mentioned a couple of times, the one thing we learn from history is that we don't learn from history. Another great saying about history is that those who don't know history are always condemned to repeat it.

We often take our cues from Solomon in thinking that we are wise enough and clever enough not to let it happen to us, as if we can live on the edge and never fall off. When we become narcissists, thinking that the world revolves around us, we are going to fail. When we think we are the center of the universe, our universe is way too small.

Just as it happened to Jeremiah himself, all of Jerusalem's supposed friends had dealt treacherously with her and had now become her enemies.[4] How often does that happen to us? People we thought were our friends end up deserting us in our time of need.

Israel had been taken into captivity by the Assyrians, and now Judah by the Babylonians. Judah dwelled among the heathen and found no rest as her persecutors overtook her between the straits.[5] I mentioned earlier about the four fast days that are mentioned in Zechariah[6] and how each of them have to do with the destruction of the temple. Here's a quick snapshot of what I'm referring to:

The fast of the tenth month is the tenth day of Tevet, when Nebuchadnezzar surrounded the city to besiege it.

The fast of the fourth month is on the seventeenth of Tammuz, when Nebuchadnezzar broke through the walls.

The fast of the fifth month is on the ninth of Av, when the temple and Jerusalem was burned to the ground.

The fast of the first month is on the second of Tishri, when Gedaliah, the governor installed by Nebuchadnezzar, was assassinated.

There are three weeks from the fast of the fourth month to the fast of the fifth month—or it could be said from the seventeenth of Tammuz, when the walls were broken down, to the ninth of Av, when the temple was destroyed. These three weeks have become known as the dire straits.

Lamentations mentions here how her persecutors overtook her between the straits. Every year this three-week time frame between these two bookend fasts is known as Bein HaMetzarim, meaning between the straits. It is a time of reflection and mourning. These two dates have been cursed throughout Jewish history, as calamities have fallen many times on these two dates. It all began with the seventeenth of Tammuz, when they worshipped the golden calf, and the ninth of Av, when the ten spies gave the slanderous report of the Promised Land.

Jerusalem had now fallen into the hands of her enemy, and there was no one there to help her.[7] Jerusalem, Israel, needed to trust in God, not in Egypt or Assyria. And the same is true prophetically today as well. While the USA needs to strongly protect Israel, ultimately Israel has to trust in God, not the United States. Our presidents come and go, along with the support of Israel.

In Zechariah we find that all nations would come against Jerusalem.[8] Not only was there no one there to help her, we also find that all of her adversaries were mocking her Sabbaths.[9] The Sabbaths were likened to her wedding ring, being in covenant with the God of Israel. God said the Sabbath was the sign of their being in covenant to each other.[10]

In Jewish circles it is said concerning the Jewish people keeping the Sabbath that it was really the Sabbaths that kept them. When they kept the Sabbaths, God protected them, and when they did not, they were judged.

Even today in some religious circles they believe if all the Jews would keep just two Sabbaths in a row, the Messiah would come. Others say it would only take one! Many believers join the enemies of Israel today and still mock the Sabbaths of Israel, along with all those who try to honor them by obeying the Lord.

Jeremiah's eyes were running down with tears because the comforter who should be relieving him was far from him.[11] We know that Messiah's generation also saw the destruction of the temple, and He too mourned the future desolation coming upon the city and upon His house because of all the wickedness going on. Unbelievably, a second time they did not realize it was the time of their visitation.[12]

This again is why we need to be on God's calendar! When we go to the Book of Acts, we find that God has an appointed time for the salvation of every nation, not just Israel.[13] If you are a prayer warrior reading this, you especially need to know the appointed times in history that are for your nation.

Yeshua knew that after He left, the destruction of the temple would come, and His people would be looking for another comforter, just as Jeremiah was, so He sent the Comforter ahead of time.[14] In Jeremiah we see Zion stretching forth her hand, looking for comfort.[15] In the Book of Romans we see the Lord speaking to Israel, declaring that all day long He had continually been stretching forth His hands to them, a disobedient and gainsaying people.[16]

In the very first chapter of Proverbs the Lord said that because He called and they refused to answer, because He stretched out His hand and no one regarded, and because they would have none of His reproof, He would laugh at their calamity and mock them when their fear came. And after distress and anguish came upon them and they called upon Him, He wouldn't answer. They would even seek Him early and still wouldn't find Him.[17] The body of Messiah today needs to learn a great lesson from this.

CHAPTER 2: THE LAW IS NO MORE TO BE SEEN

The Lord was an enemy to Israel, and just as He promised, He took away the temple just as He took away His tabernacle. All of God's appointed times, the feasts and Sabbaths held in Zion, were forgotten—mostly because of the leadership, the kings and the priests who led the people astray.[18]

From Ecclesiastes we know that God has a time and a purpose for everything under heaven.[19] The Lord purposed to destroy the wall of the daughter of Zion. Lamentations states that even her gates were sunk into the ground, her king and princes were among the Gentiles, the Law was no more, and her prophets found no vision from the Lord.[20] Again, this comment is huge!

When the Law is done away with, the prophets find no vision. In Proverbs we find that where there is no vision, the people perish.[21] When we read the rest of the verse, we find whoever keeps the Law is happy. That is because true biblical prophetic vision only came to those who keep the Law.

In Proverbs we also find that the commandment is a lamp, and the Law is light.[22] We know in the Gospels the foolish virgins' lamps went out, and the reason we now see was because they were not keeping the commandments. Where the Law is, there is not only light but also liberty![23]

Most people want to destroy the Law, but God's desire is to make it honorable and magnify it![24] All of Israel's enemies were opening their mouths, rejoicing that Israel had been defeated. This was the very day they had been joyfully waiting for, and now they had found it and seen it![25] The Bible gives a woe to anyone who desires the Day of the Lord.[26]

CHAPTER 3: LOOKING FOR THE LORD'S MERCIES

Jeremiah recalled to mind that it was because of the Lord's mercies that they were not completely consumed. Because His compassions do not fail, Jeremiah still had hope. He knew God's mercies are new every morning and He is faithful! He recalled that the Lord is always good to those who wait for Him and seek Him. Jeremiah reminds us that we should hope and quietly wait for the salvation of the Lord.[27] This is amazing to me—after all he had been through, Jeremiah cast all of his care upon the Lord because he knew that God truly cared for him. It all came down to attitude.

Many felt that God had freed them from Egypt just so He could kill them in the wilderness. This reminds me of a parable in the Gospels in which one of the master's servants was given funds to invest, and he just buried them. When it came time to report how it went, he used the excuse that he knew the master was a hard man, reaping where he didn't sow. The master called him a wicked servant and cast him into outer darkness.[28]

The question is, How do we perceive God from the very depth of our hearts? Do we really believe He is out for our good, or is He just trying to make our lives miserable? As I mentioned earlier, many ask others if they believe in God. The phrase is better asked when the word *believe* is more truly rendered as *trust*. The real question is, Do you *trust* in God.

The other day, as I was carrying on my conversation time with the Lord, He expressed to me that "He is always looking for the one that He can trust in!" It's so much more than whether you trust in God; it's whether He can trust you!

We know that even though the Lord may cause us grief, He will have compassion on us according to the multitude of His mercies because He never willingly afflicts or grieves the children of men out of spite.[29] So why is it that we complain so much when we really deserve what is coming as a result of our sins? We read that we need to search our ways, turn again to the Lord, lift up our hearts with our hands to our heavenly Father, and admit we have transgressed and rebelled.[30]

Jeremiah recalled how his enemies chased after him without a cause, throwing him into the dungeon and covering it with a stone. He had thought he was a dead man and called out to the Lord from the dungeon. And the Lord heard his cry, told him not to fear, and redeemed him.[31]

CHAPTER 4: NOT LOOKING TO THE NATIONS FOR HELP

The Lord accomplished His fury, pouring out His fierce anger and devouring the foundations of Zion. The kings of the earth and the inhabitants of the world were in unbelief that Israel's adversaries and enemies should have ever entered into the gates of Jerusalem. It was because of the sins of her prophets and the iniquities of her priests, having shed innocent blood in her midst.[32] Their eyes were failing in waiting for the help from a nation who could not save them.[33]

Jeremiah told the daughter of Edom to go ahead and rejoice and be glad because her turn was coming when she too would drink of the cup of wrath.[34] It is horrifying when we read of what Edom did to those from Judah who were trying to flee during the war with Nebuchadnezzar.

Remember that Edom refers to the nation of Esau. Esau was the brother of Jacob. Edom also broke the brotherly covenant by pursuing his brother with a sword. Edom was full of pride and consequently deceived! He was so exalted that he felt no one could bring him to back to earth, but God was going to bring him down![35] It was because of the violence he did to his brother, Jacob, when he stood on the other side while strangers carried away the captives to Babylon. When foreigners entered the gates of Jerusalem, the hearts of Edom were as the captors. They should not have looked on the day his brother was taken captive and became a stranger. They also rejoiced over the children of Judah in the day of their destruction and entered the gates to partake in the spoils. They even stood in the crossways, preventing those who were trying to escape from escaping.[36]

CHAPTER 5: THE EYES HAVE BECOME DIM

Jeremiah could not believe the situation they were in. They were as orphans and fatherless. They now had to pay to drink their own water, and their own wood was being sold to them. They were under persecution and were having to labor, finding no rest, as they were now having to put their necks under a yoke. They were reduced to begging the nations of Egypt and Assyria for bread.[37]

Jeremiah cried that the joy of their hearts had ceased, and their dancing had been turned into mourning. The crown had fallen from their heads, and woe to them for their sins. It was because of this their hearts had become faint and their eyes dimmed. The foxes were now walking upon the mountain of Zion that had become desolate.[38]

What was this crown being talked about? In Ezekiel we find that God claims to have decked Israel with all kinds of beautiful ornaments, putting bracelets on her hands, a chain around her neck, a jewel in her forehead, earrings in her ears, and a beautiful crown upon her head.[39]

When we connect these verses to Proverbs, we find that a son was to hear the instruction of his father and not to forsake the Torah of his mother because they are an ornament of grace to the head and a chains around the neck.[40] The Law was to be a beautiful jewelry chain around the neck, not the tire chain many make it out to be. The crown was the Law of God. What type of king rules according to the whims of men who throw out and trash God's gracious laws?

Jeremiah talked about the foxes running around on the Temple Mount. History repeated itself six hundred years later, when the temple was destroyed again. Rabbi Akiva and three others were looking at the devastation that had been done in 70 BC. They saw a fox running through the devastation, and the three started mourning. But Rabbi Akiva started laughing, and they asked him why. He stated that if the prophecies were true of the destruction of Jerusalem, then that meant the prophecies were also true of the restoration!

Jeremiah also spoke of their eyes being dim. We read of Isaac's eyes being dim to the point he could not tell Jacob from Esau and of his son Jacob's eyes being dim so he couldn't tell Ephraim apart from Manasseh.[41] Jacob's name got changed to the name of Israel, and we find in Romans that Israel's blindness in part has happened until the maturity of the Gentiles has come in.[42]

We know as believers that we see through a glass darkly and only know in part as well.[43] Both Jews and Gentiles see through a glass darkly, and the first group to humble themselves and look through the other's lens would be able to see the clearer picture. We both need the full-spectrum glasses that only the Messiah can give.

We close our look at the Book of Lamentations with the knowledge that the Lord remains forever and His throne from generation to generation. Jeremiah cried out, asking why the Lord had forsaken them for such a long time. He asked for the Lord to turn them that they may be turned toward Him and to renew their days as the days of old. Jeremiah closed his lament, feeling the Lord's rejection and knowing He was very angry at them.[44]

Let's summarize some thoughts.

Calamity comes when we think we are smarter than God. We must remember that when God calls, we better answer. Any prophet who proclaims God's Law is done away with is a false prophet who has no vision. We always need to be looking for the Lord's mercies, and Israel needs to always look to God for their help. Right now we see through a glass darkly and only see in part. Romans 11 says Israel also was only blinded in part. I truly believe the first group to humble themselves and look out of the other's lens will be able to see the whole picture and see it more clearly.

QUESTIONS

- What is the Lord telling you about Himself?

- What else has the Lord taught you?

CONCLUSION

A s I DUG deep into the Book of Jeremiah, trying to put the puzzle of his message back together, I could feel the heartbreak and tension, as well as his love for God and his love for the people. I could feel the chaos, smell the battles raging, sense the betrayal of people, and see how history truly repeats itself in our day. We see the chaos our world is in and how few genuinely biblical prophets are out there preaching true repentance to the body of Messiah rather than massaging the consciences of the people.

The church today is basically just as lawless as the people of God were 2,500 years ago. Like Jeremiah, many of God's servants feel all alone, with their voices being shut down not only in the political world or at their jobs but also in the church as they cry out prophetically for true repentance and a return to God. There is a cacophony of voices shouting to be heard, as anyone knows who watches television or gets on the internet.

The warnings from Jeremiah truly parallel the warnings that need to be heard in our generation today. The main encouragement we need to hold on to is that God keeps covenant and His mercies endure forever. I believe God is giving a clarion call to all who have ears to hear what He is saying to us today. As believers, now more than ever, we need to plug in where the truth is being taught and not be caught up with all the false prophetic voices preaching a false peace and saying all is well while we are lulled to sleep.

Too many pastors have become life coaches instead of fathers teaching us the responsibilities of living close to the Messiah. They are more like death coaches, teaching that the Bible is all about us rather than how to draw near to God.

God is looking for people He can trust to pour out His Spirit upon in these last days. He looks for people who are selfless, humble, and not in it for any fame, fortune, or power but want to see Him, not themselves, magnified. God is looking for warriors who realize their only interest is in advancing His kingdom by storming the gates of hell and setting His sons and daughters free from the clutches of the greatest narcissist of all times.

Jeremiah has always been my hero, and I pray this book has inspired you to take another look at his incredible life and draw closer to our great God!

NOTES

Introduction

1.   Isaiah 1:2–3.
2.   Jeremiah 25:11.
3.   Leviticus 18:25–30.
4.   Georg Wilhelm Friedrich Hegel, *Lectures on the Philosophy of World History* (Cambridge: Cambridge University Press, 1980), 21, https://books.google.com/books?id=pjfaimuprzoC&q.
5.   Ecclesiastes 1:9.
6.   Binyamin Lau, *Jeremiah the Fate of a Prophet* (New Milford, CT: Koren Publishers, 2013), xv, https://www.amazon.com/Jeremiah-Binyamin-Lau/dp/1592641946.
7.   Jeremiah 26:8.
8.   Jeremiah 38:4.
9.   Jeremiah 11:21.
10.   Jeremiah 20:10.
11.   Jeremiah 12:6.
12.   Jeremiah 16:1–2.

Chapter 1

1.   2 Kings 16:2.
2.   2 Kings 15:23–30; 17:1–5.
3.   2 Kings 16:7; 17:1–6; 18:13; 19:37.

4. Hosea 4:1–2.
5. Hosea 4:6.
6. Micah 3:12.
7. Jeremiah 26:7–19.
8. Isaiah 5:20–21.
9. Isaiah 5:24.
10. Isaiah 1:1–3.
11. Isaiah 7:1–9.
12. Isaiah 7:10–17.
13. 2 Chronicles 29:1.
14. 2 Chronicles 28:1–8.
15. 2 Chronicles 28:9–18.
16. 2 Kings 16:7–17.
17. 2 Kings 17:6.
18. 2 Kings 18:1–2.
19. 2 Chronicles 30:1–12.
20. 2 Kings 18:4–5.
21. Hosea 1:2.
22. Hosea 8:11–12.
23. Hosea 10:12.
24. Hosea 14:8–9.
25. 2 Kings 18:7–13.
26. 2 Kings 18:14–16.
27. Joshua 1:1–9.
28. 2 Chronicles 32:1–8.
29. 2 Kings 18:17–37; 2 Chronicles 32:18–20.
30. 2 Kings 18:19–25.
31. Micah 4:2–4.
32. 2 Kings 18:31.
33. 2 Kings 19:2–7.
34. 2 Kings 20:1–6.
35. 2 Kings 19:35–36.
36. 2 Kings 19:35–36.
37. 2 Chronicles 32:22–23.

38. 2 Chronicles 32:25–30.

39. 2 Chronicles 32:31.

40. Isaiah 39:1–2.

41. Isaiah 39:5–8.

42. 2 Chronicles 33:1.

43. Micah 4:1–2.

44. Micah 6:2–3.

45. Micah 6:6–7.

46. Micah 6:8.

47. Hosea 14:1.

48. 2 Chronicles 33:2–7.

49. OU Staff, "Fast of the 17th of Tammuz: Historical Background & Customs," Orthodox Union, July 18, 2011, https://www.ou.org/holidays /fast-of-shiva-asar-btammuz/the_17th_of_tammuz1/.

50. Isaiah 62:4–5.

51. Isaiah 62:6–7.

52. StudyLight.org, "Verse-by-Verse Bible Commentary: 2 Kings 21:1," accessed March 9, 2020, https://www.studylight.org/ commentary/2 -kings/21-1.html.

53. 2 Kings 21:1.

54. Hebrews 11:37–38.

55. Bible Study Tools, "Hebrews 11:37," accessed March 9, 2020, https://www.biblestudytools.com/commentaries/gills-exposition-of-the -bible/hebrews-11-37.html.

56. 2 Kings 21:10–16.

57. 2 Chronicles 33:10–11.

58. 2 Chronicles 33:12–16.

59. 2 Chronicles 33:21–25.

60. 2 Chronicles 34:1.

Chapter 2

1. 1 Kings 12:26–33.
2. 1 Kings 13:1–2.
3. 2 Chronicles 34:1–3.
4. Jeremiah 1:1–2.
5. Joshua 21:17–18.
6. Jeremiah 1:4–5.
7. Jeremiah 1:6–9.
8. Jeremiah 1:10.
9. Jeremiah 1:11–12.
10. Jeremiah 1:13–14.
11. Jeremiah 1:17–19.
12. 2 Chronicles 34:8.
13. 2 Chronicles 34:11.
14. 2 Chronicles 34:9–11.
15. 2 Kings 22:8–13.
16. 2 Kings 22:18–20.
17. 2 Kings 23:1–8.
18. 2 Kings 23:7.
19. 2 Kings 23:10.
20. 2 Kings 23:11–12.
21. 2 Kings 23:13–14.
22. 1 Kings 11:7–8.
23. Leviticus 20:1–5.
24. 1 Kings 13:1–3.
25. 2 Kings 23:15–17.
26. 2 Chronicles 35:1–19.
27. 2 Kings 23:1–3.

Chapter 3

1. Zephaniah 1:1.
2. Zephaniah 1:2–4.
3. Zephaniah 1:7–8.

4. Matthew 25:1–13.
5. Luke 12:35–40.
6. Song of Songs [or Song of Solomon] 5:2.
7. Deuteronomy 28:12.
8. Song of Songs [or Song of Solomon] 5:3–7.
9. Jeremiah 29:13.
10. Zephaniah 1:12–16.
11. Zephaniah 2:1–3.
12. Zephaniah 3:1–4.
13. Zephaniah 3:9.
14. Zephaniah 3:10–12.
15. Zephaniah 3:14–20.
16. Jeremiah 3:1.
17. Jeremiah 3:3.
18. Jeremiah 3:6–8.
19. Ezekiel 16:46–47.
20. Jeremiah 3:10–11.
21. Jeremiah 3:12–14.
22. Jeremiah 14:1–4.
23. Jeremiah 14:11–12.
24. Jeremiah 14:13–16.
25. Matthew 7:22–23.
26. Jeremiah 14:17–18.

CHAPTER 4

1. Isaiah 29:13.
2. Ezekiel 33:32.
3. Jeremiah 17:1–4.
4. Jeremiah 17:5–8.
5. Psalm 139:23–24.
6. Jeremiah 17:9–10.
7. John 7:37–38.
8. John 7:45–49.

9.   Psalm 119:97, 113, 163, 165.
10.   John 8:3–9.
11.   Jeremiah 17:21–25.
12.   Jeremiah 17:27.
13.   Jeremiah 11:1–8.
14.   Deuteronomy 27:26.
15.   Jeremiah 11:11–12.
16.   Jeremiah 11:14.
17.   Jeremiah 11:19.
18.   Jeremiah 11:20.
19.   Jeremiah 11:21–23.
20.   Jeremiah 12:1–2.
21.   Jeremiah 12:3–4.
22.   Jeremiah 12:5–6.
23.   Ezekiel 33:30–32.
24.   James 1:21–25.
25.   Jeremiah 12:7–11.
26.   Jeremiah 12:14–15.
27.   Jeremiah 12:16–17.
28.   Jeremiah 9:1–3.
29.   Jeremiah 9:4–5.
30.   Jeremiah 9:8–9.
31.   Jeremiah 9:13–16.
32.   Jeremiah 9:23–24.
33.   Jeremiah 9:25–26.

CHAPTER 5

1.   Jeremiah 15:1.
2.   Jeremiah 15:3–4.
3.   Leviticus 26:1–8.
4.   Leviticus 26:16–17.
5.   Leviticus 26:21–22.
6.   Leviticus 26:23–26.

7.	Leviticus 26:27–30.
8.	Leviticus 26:32–35.
9.	Deuteronomy 15:1–3.
10.	Jeremiah 34:12–22.
11.	Jeremiah 15:7.
12.	Matthew 3:11–12.
13.	Matthew 13:24–30.
14.	1 Chronicles 21:15–26.
15.	Luke 17:34–37.
16.	Zechariah 14:16–19.
17.	Revelation 19:11–19.
18.	Jeremiah 16:10–13.
19.	Jeremiah 16:14–17.
20.	Matthew 4:19.
21.	Jeremiah 16:19–21.
22.	Habakkuk 1:1–4.
23.	Luke 17:26–30.
24.	Genesis 6:11–13.
25.	Habakkuk 1:5–7.
26.	Habakkuk 2:2–4.
27.	Habakkuk 2:14.
28.	Habakkuk 3:17–19.

CHAPTER 6

1.	Jeremiah 7:3–7.
2.	Jeremiah 7:8–11.
3.	Matthew 21:12–13.
4.	Jeremiah 7:12–14.
5.	Jeremiah 7:21–24; Exodus 19:5–6.
6.	Jeremiah 7:25–27.
7.	Jeremiah 7:30–31.
8.	Matthew 18:1–10.
9.	Jeremiah 18:5–8.

10.   Jeremiah 18:15.

11.   Jeremiah 18:18.

12.   Jeremiah 18:19–23.

13.   Jeremiah 19:1–6.

14.   1 Samuel 3:11–14.

15.   2 Kings 21:10–12.

16.   Jeremiah 19:10–13.

17.   Jeremiah 19:14–15.

18.   Jeremiah 2:4–6.

19.   Deuteronomy 1:30–31.

20.   Jeremiah 2:8.

21.   Deuteronomy 33:10.

22.   Malachi 2:4–8.

23.   Revelation 3:20.

24.   Jeremiah 2:13.

25.   Jeremiah 2:18; Lamentations 5:6.

26.   Jeremiah 2:22–23.

27.   Jeremiah 2:26–28.

28.   Jeremiah 2:32.

29.   Jeremiah 2:35.

30.   John 9:41.

31.   Nahum 1:1–3.

32.   Nahum 3:1.

33.   2 Chronicles 35:20–21.

34.   2 Chronicles 35:22–25.

35.   2 Kings 23:28–30.

36.   2 Kings 23:31–35.

37.   2 Kings 23:36.

38.   2 Kings 23:36.

CHAPTER 7

1.   Jeremiah 26:1–3.

2.   Jeremiah 26:4–6.

3.   "The Destruction of the Tabernacle of Shiloh," Jewish Bible Quarterly, accessed March 18, 2020, https://jbqnew.jewishbible.org/jbq
-past-issues/2016/441-january-march-2016/reconstructing-
destruction
-tabernacle-shiloh/.

4.   Jeremiah 26:7–9.

5.   Jeremiah 26:10–11.

6.   Jeremiah 26:12.

7.   Jeremiah 26:13–15.

8.   Jeremiah 26:16–19.

9.   Jeremiah 26:20–24.

10.   2 Kings 22:8–10.

11.   Jeremiah 39:14; 2 Kings 25:25.

12.   Jeremiah 27:1–3.

13.   Jeremiah 25:1–3.

14.   Jeremiah 25:4–12; Deuteronomy 28:36–37.

15.   Jeremiah 25:12–15.

16.   Revelation 14:8–10.

17.   Jeremiah 25:17–29.

18.   Jeremiah 25:30.

19.   Jeremiah 25:32–33.

CHAPTER 8

1.   Jeremiah 22:1–5.

2.   Jeremiah 22:8–12.

3.   Jeremiah 22:15–17.

4.   Jeremiah 9:23–24.

5.   Jeremiah 22:24–28.

6.   Jeremiah 22:30.

7.   Matthew 1:12.

8.   Haggai 2:1–9.

9.   John 7:37.

10. Jeremiah 36:1–2.
11. Jeremiah 36:3.
12. Jeremiah 36:4–8.
13. Jeremiah 4:6–8.
14. Joel 1:14–15.
15. Joel 2:1.
16. Joel 2:12–13.
17. Joel 2:17 .
18. Jeremiah 45:3, NKJV.
19. Jeremiah 45:1–5.
20. Jeremiah 36:9.
21. Jeremiah 36:10–19.
22. Jeremiah 36:20–21.
23. Jeremiah 36:22–24.
24. Daniel 2:1.
25. Daniel 3:21–25.
26. Song of Solomon 8:9; Proverbs 26:14.
27. John 10:9.
28. Jeremiah 23:29.
29. Jeremiah 36:26–32.

Chapter 9

1. Jeremiah 13:1–7.
2. Jeremiah 13:8–11.
3. Jeremiah 13:12–14.
4. E.g., Revelation 2:7, NKJV.
5. Jeremiah 13:15–16.
6. Jeremiah 13:17.
7. Jeremiah 13:18.
8. Proverbs 16:18–19.
9. Jeremiah 35:1–5.
10. Jeremiah 35:6–11.
11. Jeremiah 35:12–16.

12.   Jeremiah 35:18–19.

13.   2 Kings 10:11–15.

14.   2 Kings 10:17–28.

15.   Judges 1:16; 1 Chronicles 2:55. See also commentary by Rashi on Numbers 10:32, Chabad, accessed March 11, 2020, https://www.chabad .org/library/bible_cdo/aid/9938/jewish/Chapter-10.htm/showrashi/ true.

16.   *Fausset's Bible Dictionary*, s.v. "Rechab," StudyLight.org, accessed March 11, 2020, https://www.studylight.org/dictionaries/ fbd/r/rechab.html.

17.   *Fausset's Bible Dictionary*, s.v. "Rechab."

18.   "The Death of James the Just, Brother of Jesus Christ," Christian History for Everyman, accessed March 18, 2020, https:// www.christian -history.org/death-of-james.html.

CHAPTER 10

1.   2 Kings 24:1.

2.   Jeremiah 4:1–4.

3.   Hosea 10:12.

4.   Matthew 13:22.

5.   Jeremiah 4:5–8.

6.   Jeremiah 4:9–10.

7.   Jeremiah 4:22.

8.   Lau, *Jeremiah the Fate of a Prophet*, xv–xvii.

9.   Jeremiah 5:1.

10.   Jeremiah 5:7.

11.   Deuteronomy 8:10.

12.   Leviticus 25:1–11.

13.   Leviticus 25:20–22.

14.   Jeremiah 5:11–14.

15.   Jeremiah 5:15–22.

16. Jeremiah 5:23–26.

17. Jeremiah 5:30–31.

18. Jeremiah 6:10–15.

19. Jeremiah 6:16–17.

20. Matthew 11:28–30.

21. John 14:6.

22. Psalm 119:1.

23. Psalm 119:142.

24. Proverbs 13:14; 6:23.

25. Jeremiah 8:5–6.

26. Jeremiah 8:7–9.

27. Jeremiah 8:10–11.

28. Jeremiah 10:1–4.

29. Jeremiah 10:22.

30. Jeremiah 6:14; 8:11.

Chapter 11

1. Jeremiah 23:1–4.

2. Jeremiah 23:5–6.

3. Jeremiah 23:7–8.

4. Jeremiah 23:9–12.

5. Luke 19:43–44.

6. Ecclesiastes 3:1–2.

7. Amos 3:3.

8. Jeremiah 23:14.

9. Robert Barron, *Letter to a Suffering Church: A Bishop Speaks on the Sexual Abuse Crisis* (Park Ridge, IL: Word on Fire, 2019), 8.

10. Barron, *Letter to a Suffering Church*, 50.

11. Jeremiah 23:19–20.

12. Jeremiah 23:20.

13. Isaiah 55:11.

14. Jeremiah 23:21–22.

15.   Ecclesiastes 8:11.
16.   Jeremiah 23:23–27.
17.   Song of Solomon 2:14–15.
18.   Ezekiel 13:4.
19.   Jeremiah 23:28–32.
20.   Jeremiah 23:33.
21.   Jeremiah 23:36.
22.   Jeremiah 23:39–40.
23.   2 Kings 24:5–7.
24.   Daniel 1:1.
25.   Jeremiah 25:1.
26.   2 Kings 24:1.
27.   2 Kings 24:10–13.
28.   2 Kings 24:14–17.
29.   2 Chronicles 36:9.
30.   2 Kings 24:8.
31.   Jeremiah 52:28.
32.   Esther 2:5–6.
33.   Esther 2:16.
34.   Ezra 2:1–2.
35.   Jeremiah 52:29.
36.   Jeremiah 52:30.

CHAPTER 12

1.   Jeremiah 30:1–3.
2.   Jeremiah 30:6–7.
3.   Mark 13:8.
4.   Jeremiah 30:10–11.
5.   Jeremiah 30:18–19.
6.   Jeremiah 30:23–24.
7.   Jeremiah 31:1–6.
8.   Jeremiah 31:7–11.
9.   Jeremiah 31:12–13.

10.   Jeremiah 31:15.

11.   Matthew 2:16–18.

12.   Jeremiah 31:16–20.

13.   Daniel 7:13–14.

14.   Ezekiel 37:16–17.

15.   Jeremiah 31:27–28.

16.   Amos 9:15.

17.   Jeremiah 31:21.

18.   Jeremiah 31:31.

19.   Jeremiah 31:31–33.

20.   Ezekiel 36:26–27.

21.   Jeremiah 31:34–37.

22.   2 Chronicles 36:11–13.

23.   2 Chronicles 36:14–15.

24.   2 Chronicles 36:16.

25.   Matthew 21:33–39.

26.   Jeremiah 24:1–10.

27.   Jeremiah 29:1.

28.   Jeremiah 29:3–7.

29.   Jeremiah 29:8–13.

30.   Jeremiah 29:20–21.

31.   Jeremiah 29:30–32.

Chapter 13

1.   Jeremiah 46:10.

2.   Jeremiah 46:13–17.

3.   Jeremiah 46:25–28.

4.   Jeremiah 47:1–4.

5.   Jeremiah 48:1.

6.   Deuteronomy 34:1.

7.   Jeremiah 48:7.

8.   Genesis 11:27; 19:36–37.

9.   Jeremiah 48:10.

10. Matthew 7:21–23.

11. Jeremiah 48:25–30.

12. Jeremiah 49:1, NKJV.

13. Jeremiah 49:1–2.

14. Jeremiah 49:7–8.

15. Jeremiah 49:13–18.

16. Isaiah 63:1–4.

17. Revelation 19:11–15.

18. Leviticus 16:17–19.

19. Revelation 15:5–8.

20. Revelation 11:15–19.

21. Leviticus 16:12–13.

22. Psalm 141:2.

23. Revelation 8:3–5.

24. Jeremiah 50:1–2.

25. Jeremiah 50:4–7.

26. "Prophetic News," The Prophetic Scroll, accessed March 18, 2020, http://thepropheticscroll.org/home/?deca3cf7465d64766077d 9cbda37875a=32565f75dce7dea8a313194fdf6293e4&start=425.

27. John Hagee, *In Defense of Israel, Revised and Updated* (Lake Mary, FL: FrontLine, 2007), 133.

28. "Why Lucifer/Satan Hates the Jews—1," Fivedoves.com, accessed March 18, 2020, http://www.fivedoves.com/letters/ june2014/pastorbob622-5.htm.

29. Revelation 14:1.

30. Revelation 7:4–8.

31. Revelation 7:9.

32. Jeremiah 50:9.

33. Isaiah 21:3–9.

34. Jeremiah 50:15.

35. Revelation 14:8.

36. Revelation 18:1–2.

37. Jeremiah 50:17–20.

38. Jeremiah 50:33–34.

39.   Jeremiah 50:40–43.
40.   Jeremiah 51:5–9.
41.   Revelation 18:2–6.
42.   Jeremiah 51:11.
43.   Jeremiah 51:16.
44.   Revelation 1:15.
45.   Jeremiah 51:20–24.
46.   Jeremiah 51:42.
47.   Jeremiah 51:45.
48.   Jeremiah 51:59–64.
49.   Revelation 18:21.

Chapter 14

1.   Jeremiah 28:1.
2.   Jeremiah 27:2–6.
3.   Jeremiah 27:8–11.
4.   Jeremiah 27:12–18.
5.   Jeremiah 27:19–22.
6.   Jeremiah 28:1–4.
7.   Jeremiah 28:5–6.
8.   Jeremiah 28:7–9.
9.   Jeremiah 28:10–11.
10.   Jeremiah 28:12–17.
11.   Revelation 2:10.
12.   Jeremiah 21:1–2.
13.   Jeremiah 21:3–7.
14.   Jeremiah 21:8–12.
15.   Jeremiah 20:1–4.
16.   Jeremiah 20:5–6.
17.   Jeremiah 20:7–9.
18.   Jeremiah 20:10.
19.   Jeremiah 20:11.
20.   Jeremiah 20:13–18.

21. Jeremiah 37:3–5.
22. Jeremiah 37:6–10.
23. Jeremiah 37:11–17.
24. Jeremiah 37:18–21.
25. Ezekiel 1:28.
26. Ezekiel 2:1–2.
27. Ezekiel 2:3–5.
28. Ezekiel 2:8–10.
29. Ezekiel 3:1–3.
30. Revelation 10:9–10.
31. Ezekiel 8:1.
32. Ezekiel 8:2–4.
33. Ezekiel 8:5–16.
34. Ezekiel 9:1–4.
35. Ezekiel 10:4.
36. Ezekiel 10:18–19.
37. Ezekiel 11:1–13.
38. Ezekiel 11:22–23.
39. Acts 1:9–12.
40. Ezekiel 20:1.
41. Jeremiah 34:1–2.
42. Deuteronomy 15:1–18.
43. Deuteronomy 31:10–13.
44. Jeremiah 34:8–11.
45. Jeremiah 34:12–17.
46. Jeremiah 34:22.

Chapter 15

1. Jeremiah 33:1–3.
2. Jeremiah 33:4–8.
3. Jeremiah 33:9–11, NKJV.
4. Jeremiah 33:12–15.
5. Jeremiah 33:16–18.

6.   Jeremiah 33:19–22.
7.   Jeremiah 33:23–26.
8.   Jeremiah 38:1–5.
9.   1 Samuel 15:24.
10. Jeremiah 38:6–13.
11. Jeremiah 38:14–18.
12. Jeremiah 38:19.
13. Jeremiah 38:20–28.
14. 2 Kings 25:1–2.
15. Ezekiel 24:1–6.
16. Zechariah 8:19.
17. Jeremiah 32:1–3.
18. Jeremiah 32:6–8.
19. Jeremiah 32:16–17.
20. Jeremiah 32:21–23.
21. Jeremiah 32:32–33.
22. Jeremiah 32:34–35.
23. Jeremiah 32:37–42.
24. Ezekiel 29:1–3.
25. Ezekiel 30:20–22.
26. Ezekiel 31:1–2.
27. Ezekiel 32:1–16.
28. Ezekiel 33:21.
29. Ezekiel 33:30–33.

CHAPTER 16

1.   Jeremiah 39:2–4.
2.   Jeremiah 39:5–7; 52:11.
3.   Jeremiah 39:8–14.
4.   2 Kings 22:8.
5.   Jeremiah 26:24.
6.   Jeremiah 39:15–18.
7.   Jeremiah 40:2–3.

8.   Jeremiah 40:4–6.

9.   Jeremiah 40:7–9.

10.   Jeremiah 40:11–12.

11.   Jeremiah 40:15–16.

12.   Jeremiah 41:1–3; 2 Kings 25:25.

13.   Jeremiah 41:10–14.

14.   Jeremiah 42:1–3.

15.   Jeremiah 42:4–6.

16.   Jeremiah 42:7–12.

17.   Jeremiah 42:13–19.

18.   Jeremiah 42:20–22.

19.   Jeremiah 43:1–4.

20.   Exodus 13:17; Deuteronomy 17:16.

21.   Jeremiah 43:5–6.

22.   Jeremiah 43:7–12.

Chapter 17

1.   Jeremiah 44:1–3.

2.   Leviticus 18:26–28; 20:22.

3.   Jeremiah 44:4–8.

4.   Jeremiah 44:8–11.

5.   Jeremiah 44:15–19.

6.   Jeremiah 44:20–23.

7.   Jeremiah 44:24–30.

8.   Ezekiel 40:1.

9.   Ezekiel 40:2–3.

10.   Ezekiel 43:1–2.

11.   Ezekiel 48:31–34.

12.   Revelation 21:10–27.

13.   Jeremiah 52:31–34.

CHAPTER 18

1. Lamentations 1:1.
2. Lamentations 1:1.
3. Ezekiel 16:11–22.
4. Lamentations 1:2.
5. Lamentations 1:3.
6. Zechariah 8:19.
7. Lamentations 1:7.
8. Zechariah 14:2.
9. Lamentations 1:7.
10. Exodus 31:13–14.
11. Lamentations 1:16.
12. Luke 19:41–44.
13. Acts 17:26–27.
14. John 14:15–18.
15. Lamentations 1:17.
16. Romans 10:21.
17. Proverbs 1:24–28.
18. Lamentations 2:5–6.
19. Ecclesiastes 3:1.
20. Lamentations 2:8–9.
21. Proverbs 29:18.
22. Proverbs 6:23.
23. Psalm 119:45.
24. Isaiah 42:21.
25. Lamentations 2:16.
26. Amos 5:18.
27. Lamentations 3:21–26.
28. Matthew 25:14–30.
29. Lamentations 3:32–33.
30. Lamentations 3:39–42.
31. Lamentations 3:52–58.
32. Lamentations 4:11–13.

33. Lamentations 4:17.
34. Lamentations 4:21–22.
35. Obadiah 1–4.
36. Obadiah 10–14.
37. Lamentations 5:3–6.
38. Lamentations 5:15–18.
39. Ezekiel 16:11–12.
40. Proverbs 1:8–9.
41. Genesis 27:1; 48:10.
42. Romans 11:25.
43. 1 Corinthians 13:12.
44. Lamentations 5:19–22.

I'M SO HAPPY YOU READ MY BOOK.

I hope this book encourages you to persevere in your faith despite cultural shifts and pressures.

AS MY WAY OF SAYING THANK YOU, I AM OFFERING YOU A FREE GIFT:

- E-book: *Decoding the Antichrist and the End Times*

To get this **FREE GIFT**, please go to:
www.Biltzbook.com/gift

Thanks again and God bless you,

Mark Biltz